JOHN FORD

AND THE DRAMA OF HIS TIME

JOHN FORD

AND THE DRAMA
OF HIS TIME

Clifford Leech
Professor of English Language and
Literature in the University of Durham

1957
CHATTO & WINDUS
LONDON

Published by
Chatto & Windus Ltd
42 William IV Street
London, W.C. 2

★

Clarke, Irwin & Co. Ltd
Toronto

Printed in Great Britain by
T. and A. Constable Ltd

Contents

*

5

Contents

PREFACE

A CRITIC who to-day concerns himself with Ford must be dependent on much that he has learned from previous workers in this field: I am particularly conscious of a debt to Miss M. Joan Sargeaunt's *John Ford* (Oxford, 1935) and to Professor Robert Davril's *Le Drame de John Ford* (Paris, 1954).

The following study is based on a series of lectures given at the Shakespeare Summer School of the University of Birmingham, held at the Shakespeare Institute, Stratford-upon-Avon, in 1955. At that time I had not been able to see either Professor Davril's book or Mr H. J. Oliver's *The Problem of John Ford* (Melbourne, 1955). In revising and considerably extending the original lectures (without modifying the main lines of argument), I have freely referred to the views of both these scholars. In its plan the present study differs from previous studies of the dramatist, and this may justify its appearance despite the recency of Professor Davril's and Mr Oliver's books. My concern has not been with biography or with detailed criticism of individual plays. It has, rather, been my primary wish to throw light on Ford's genius by tracing in his work the emergence of types of dramatic writing highly characteristic of their author, and to bring out their distinguishing marks by presenting them in relation to dominant dramatic types in the drama of the Jacobean and Caroline years.

In footnotes the following abbreviations have been used throughout:

Davril=Robert Davril, *Le Drame de John Ford*, Paris, 1954.

Ewing=S. Blaine Ewing, *Burtonian Melancholy in the Plays of John Ford* (*Princeton Studies in English*), Princeton, 1940.

7

Gifford-Dyce= *The Works of John Ford*, edited by William Gifford with additions by Rev. Alexander Dyce, 1895.

Oliver=H. J. Oliver, *The Problem of John Ford*, Melbourne, 1955.

Sargeaunt=M. Joan Sargeaunt, *John Ford*, Oxford, 1935.

Sensabaugh=G. F. Sensabaugh, *The Tragic Muse of John Ford*, Stanford University, 1944.

Quotations from Ford's writings are made from the following editions:

(1) The original editions of the non-dramatic writings;

(2) *The Queen: or The Excellency of her Sex*, edited by W. Bang (*Materialen zur Kunde des älteren englischen Dramas*, xiii), Louvain, 1907;

(3) *The Spanish Gipsy*, in *Representative English Comedies*, iii, edited by C. M. Gayley, 1914;

(4) Gifford-Dyce for all the plays apart from *The Queen* and *The Spanish Gipsy*.

C. L.

Durham

Beginnings

BEGINNINGS

IT is probable that when *Hamlet* was first acted John Ford
was fifteen years of age. He himself came late to the writing
of plays, and his period of major activity in the theatre dates
from some ten years after Shakespeare's death. This degree
of proximity between the two dramatists makes it peculiarly
profitable to observe their different handlings of tragic
themes. Ford learned much, of course, from Shakespeare,
but only in one play, *'Tis Pity She's a Whore*, which may
have been his first independent work for the theatre,[1] did he
attempt to reproduce the tragic manner of the opening
years of the century. In that play the characterization is
complex in the Jacobean fashion: Giovanni is hero and
villain, arousing at once sympathy and revulsion, led by
fate or circumstance to a catastrophe that is both a punishment for sin and a predestined doom. We are bound to
regard Giovanni as we regard Macbeth or Webster's Vittoria
Corombona, seasoning our admiration with horror, our
horror with a sense of kinship. It may be that this is Ford's
best play: certainly it is the one that most easily wins the
attention of the reader who first knows his Shakespeare.
But it is not Ford's most characteristic play. What we shall
find in *Perkin Warbeck* and *The Broken Heart* and *Love's
Sacrifice* is a presentation of exalted human beings whose
actions never come within the scope of censure. Suffering,
not action, is the dominant strain in their world, the suffering
of melancholy or of deprivation. It is a suffering that comes
to life through the experience of a fugitive happiness, for
this dramatist has few equals in the perception of an intense
joy. And in two other ways he avoids the mere relaxation

[1] See below, p. 49.

of the pathetic: his most impressive characters have an aristocratic code of endurance, remembering always in their anguish that they are courtiers and princes; and they have a gift of words that is eloquent and yet easy, never over-sharp or over-packed, never obscure, never prolix. Ford's poetry is the poetry of an ideal court, a court dignified above that of James or Charles. All these things can be briefly illustrated from a speech near the end of *The Broken Heart*. At the court of Sparta there is a formal celebration of a wedding, and Calantha the Princess has joined in the dance. To her there come successive messengers, reporting the deaths of the King her father, of her friend Penthea, of her lover Ithocles. She appears to give no attention, and in each instance lets the dance proceed. Then she gives directions for her coronation, and after the rites in the temple she orders the affairs of her kingdom, appoints her successor, and then turns to the dead body of Ithocles:

> now I turn to thee, thou shadow
> Of my contracted lord! Bear witness all,
> I put my mother['s] wedding-ring upon
> His finger; 'twas my father's last bequest.
> Thus I new-marry him whose wife I am;
> Death shall not separate us. O, my lords,
> I but deceiv'd your eyes with antic gesture,
> When one news straight came huddling on another
> Of death! and death! and death! still I danc'd forward;
> But it struck home, and here, and in an instant.
> Be such mere women, who with shrieks and outcries
> Can vow a present end to all their sorrows,
> Yet live to court new pleasures, and outlive them:
> They are the silent griefs which cut the heart-strings;
> Let me die smiling. (V, iii.)

She is proud of her aristocratic status: she is not one of the 'mere women' who will proclaim their grief and recover from it quickly. Then she calls for a dirge to be sung, and dies as she hears it. There is no violence in her language, no blanket of the dark, no everlasting cold. Hers is the voice of a princess, not of a player-poet. No words could be more seemly for a lady whose love is dead. Yet the strangeness of Ford's power is that we believe in her love and her broken heart. He could give authority and credibility to the simplified dramatic language of Charles's time. Calantha is more symbol than woman, yet she and her gestures and her speech command our homage.

The aristocratic code in Ford—which in a democratic age may seem mere snobbishness—is a product of the 'private' theatres of his time. From about 1610 we find the development in London of two theatrical publics. The King's men acquired the small Blackfriars theatre towards the end of the first decade of the seventeenth century, using it as their winter house and for a time keeping the large, unroofed Globe for the summer. From then onwards, but especially during Charles I's reign, the people of the court and those near to them in rank formed the audience for the so-called 'private' theatres, while the lower reaches of society were found in the larger and cheaper 'public' theatres—the Red Bull, the Fortune, and the rest. Increasingly, the plays of some distinction were written for the smaller, the courtly audience. Shakespeare had written for all men, at least in his plays of the first magnitude, but Ford wrote for men and women who might dream of dying with the upper-class dignity of Ithocles and Calantha. In the 'century of the common man' we may be affronted by the notion of this, yet we shall, I think, find it difficult to remain affronted when we enter the world of *The Broken Heart*. Ford can make us accept that world's values, as we can accept those of Dante's four-fold universe or those of Spenser's fairy land. This is not, however, a matter of an attempted hypnosis which we should resist: there is, after all, something commendable in the aristocratic ideal, as there is in Dante's cosmology or Spenser's moral system.

It has been alleged, notably by Professor G. F. Sensabaugh,[1] that this dramatist is 'modern' in his antinomianism, in his attribution of all human ill to psychological causes. Certainly it would be idle to deny that Ford sees much evil caused by psychological disturbance, that in his most striking plays the individual has not much power to make a right choice, to put his affairs in order, to win safety or success. He knew Burton's *Anatomy of Melancholy* as a writer of to-day may know Freud, and could equate evil and illness. But we shall, I think, see that only in '*Tis Pity She's a Whore* does he come near to the dangerous thoughts characteristic of Webster and Chapman and implicit even in Shakespeare. Far from being antinomian, he shows at times a simple belief in Providence, he cherishes the virtues of love and fidelity and submission to a higher will,[2] he has affinities with Calvinism in his notion of an aristocratic elect. And for the elect there was not only a capacity for suffering and dying well: there could even be, on occasion, a cure for this world's ills, an establishment of a happy condition. *The Lover's Melancholy*, *The Queen* and *The Lady's Trial* all end with fortune's smile. Here again we must recognize the influence of Burton's *Anatomy of Melancholy* on the dramatist. At times he was preoccupied with incurable woe, and then he saw the human situation as tragic, the human being as capable of a mere exaltation of mien as he endured his derangement or deprivation. At other times, in other 'cases', he was conscious of the possibility of cure, and could then rejoice in the physician's skill, as in *The Lover's Melancholy* and *The Queen*, or in the patient's resoluteness in confronting and defeating the distressful situation, as in *The Lady's Trial*.

A commonplace of Ford-criticism is to draw attention to his frequent and crude use of a comic sub-plot, invariably

[1] Sensabaugh, p. 190 *et passim*.

[2] See Peter Ure, 'Marriage and the Domestic Drama in Heywood and Ford', *English Studies*, xxxii (1951), 200-16, for the orthodoxy of Ford's attitude to marriage in *The Broken Heart*.

seen as a serious blemish on his plays. When Maeterlinck translated *'Tis Pity She's a Whore*,[1] he excised the comic story of Bergetto, his casual wooing and his absurd death, and certainly for a present-day audience the play gains from the excision. Yet Ford's maladroit comedy is not a mere inheritance from the Elizabethans and the Jacobeans. S. P. Sherman would excuse the dramatist by reference to his audience: 'Some sacrifice had to be made to the ribald groundlings,'[2] he says, but there were no 'groundlings' at the Phoenix or the Blackfriars. Though bawdry and farce were well-liked by the Caroline gentry, they were not demanded. Indeed, one of Ford's best-known plays, *The Broken Heart*, has nothing of the cruder element. It is evident, I think, that he presented his comic characters as foils to the nobility, his elect. This appears most notably in *The Fancies Chaste and Noble*. There we are told of the impotent Octavio, who cherishes the arts of love though he must be only a connoisseur, not a practitioner. He keeps, therefore, a bower of beauties whose sight and speech will give him pleasure:

> To look upon fresh beauties, to discourse
> In an unblushing merriment of words,
> To hear them play or sing, and see them dance;
> To pass the time in pretty amorous questions,
> Read a chaste verse of love, or prattle riddles,
> Is th' height of his temptations. (II, ii.)

He shows, moreover, discrimination in his recruitment of the 'Fancies':

> His choices are not of the courtly train
> Nor city's practice; but the country's innocence;
> Such as are gentle-born, not meanly; such

[1] *Annabella ('Tis pity she's a whore) drame en cinq actes de John Ford traduit et adapté pour le théâtre de l'Œuvre*, Paris 1895.
[2] 'Forde's Contribution to the Decadence of the Drama', *John Fordes Dramatische Werke*, edited by W. Bang, i (1908), p. vii (*Materialen zur Kunde des älteren englischen Dramas*, Louvain, xxiii).

> To whom both gaudiness and ape-like fashions
> Are monstrous; such as cleanliness and decency
> Prompt to a virtuous envy; such as study
> A knowledge of no danger but themselves. (II, ii.)

The situation in this play is a repellent one, and we shall see later how Ford in his last Act dissolved it all in pretence,[1] but when it is displayed to us in the earlier scenes we are made to compare Octavio's perverted and yet dignified courtliness with the degrading comedy provided by his servants: they have a pretended eunuch among them, and an amorous beldam, and their talk is scabrous in the extreme. Theirs is a lower order of being, as Octavio's is indubitably a higher order. A similar, though less gross, contrast is found in the history play *Perkin Warbeck*. There the pretender Warbeck moves slowly to his defeat and the scaffold, acting most royally in all his dealings with men, winning the devoted love of Lady Katherine Gordon, and steadfastly refusing, even at the cost of life, to admit that he is an impostor: he has come to believe in his pretence, as Giovanni in *'Tis Pity She's a Whore* almost came to believe in the rightness of his love for Annabella. Warbeck indeed shows no bravery in battle: it is only in encounters where word and gesture suffice that he is master: that is sufficient for him to gain entry among Ford's nobility. But grouped around him are a number of low-born and low-mannered followers, stupidly ambitious, food for laughter and contempt. The contrast points the dramatist's effect, the low comedy ensuring our esteem for Warbeck as for Giovanni and Octavio.

It would be pointless to wish that Ford had been a more skilful comic writer, for he could not have come close enough in sympathy or understanding to make good comedy out of those of base carriage. A dramatist may despise the objects of his comic wit and manipulation, as frequently Ben Jonson does, and still contrive a feast of

---

[1] See below, p. 113.

laughter. But he must not see them as belonging to an inferior species, he must recognize them at least as his own poor relations. Ford could not do that: he was, in his independent plays, too fully the writer for the highest stratum of society, fashioning ideals for that small group, raising to a higher pitch that group's preoccupation with itself. Professor Alfred Harbage has contrasted the two types of London theatre in the early seventeenth century: on the one hand there was, he says, the 'Theatre of a Nation', with a large and varied audience, with plays broadly based on popular ideas, on themes and situations generally valid; on the other there was the 'Theatre of a Coterie', limited in its appeal to a small section of society, reflecting a minority view and often a minority's disruptiveness.[1] The picture presented by Professor Harbage is altogether too neat, for plays might pass from the public to the private theatre and vice versa, and many public plays have the self-consciousness and the satiric impulse that Professor Harbage finds characteristic of the coterie-drama. But at least we can recognize in Ford the supreme example of a dramatist with a narrow ambience, with which he developed a close sympathy. This limited him, as we have seen. He wanted the contrast of comedy with high seriousness, but his preoccupation with courtliness of behaviour closed to him the road of comic perception. Yet we must recognize that only through this exclusiveness could he have come to the point where a Princess Calantha could be imagined. There is indeed an exceptional purity in his power of imagination. This may perhaps be seen most clearly if we compare the leading figures in his plays with those in the heroic dramas of the Restoration. Dryden can present an Almanzor, a Don Sebastian, with verve and skill: he can rouse us to wonder at them, to follow their fortunes with excitement, but he cannot—even when we are most under his spell—make us believe in them. It is too evident, in fact, that he himself does

[1] *Shakespeare and the Rival Traditions*, New York 1952, *passim*.

not believe, that his heroes are manifestations of a desired but not fully imagined ideal. But in Ford there is belief, there is imagination almost unqualified. If, as at moments in *The Broken Heart*, there is a hint of doubt,[1] it is no more than is necessary for us to accept the sincerity of the belief. His limitation of outlook is the very source of his strength. We may wish that he had not attempted to reinforce his effect by a comic admixture, but it is idle to wish that he had managed it better. In no major country to-day is aristocracy a confessed ideal. But we shall understand our own past better, and perhaps a suppressed strain in ourselves, if we can recognize the strength of that ideal as well as its narrowness. In the plays of Ford we have the head and the tail of the matter.

Of his life we know little. He was born in Devonshire, and at the age of sixteen, in 1602, he was admitted to the Middle Temple. He was on occasion in trouble with the authorities, even to the point of temporary expulsion for failure to pay his buttery bill, but he was residing in the Temple as late as 1617. Probably he practised law in some capacity during his years of early manhood, though the records indicate that he was never called to the bar.[2] We have no certain evidence that he wrote for the theatre until the 1620s, but several times before that he published small works in prose and verse: none of these shows a distinctive talent, but in different ways they hint at ideas and sympathies that appeared more clearly and more finely in the plays that followed.

Perhaps the earliest of these writings was an elegy on Charles Mountjoy, Earl of Devonshire—*Fames Memoriall, or The Earle of Deuonshire Deceased: With his honourable life, peacefull end, and solemne Funerall*, published in 1606. In dedicating this poem to the Countess of Devonshire, Ford speaks of his 'vnfeathered Muse' and of his labours being 'hitherto confined to the Innes of Courte studyes much

---

[1] See below, p. 90.   [2] Sargeaunt, pp. 2-16.

18

differente'. But, though only twenty years of age and an untried poet, he prefixed to the elegy some verses addressed '*To each affected Reader*' in which his indifference to the taste of the 'many' is proclaimed. In the poem itself the dead Earl is praised for his conduct in arms, his aptitude for philosophy and his distinction as a lover. Mountjoy had married Penelope, Lady Rich, when her first husband was living: she had been divorced in the ecclesiastical courts, and the future Archbishop Laud was persuaded to perform a marriage ceremony for her and the Earl; but the marriage was declared illegal, Laud found that it stood in the way of his preferment, and 'sad disgrace', in Ford's words, fell on the Countess. When to this is added the extreme unhappiness of Lady Rich in her first marriage, it is not surprising that the man who was to write *The Broken Heart* found the subject of his elegy attractive and gave a special stress to his love-theme. The cult of aristocracy shows itself here, as he finds the elect—'Free spirits', as he calls them—especially subject to love's thraldom:

> Actiuity abroad, daliance in chambers,
> Becomes a perfect courtier, such was he,
> What mayden breast so nice, as locks of amber
> Could not inchant with loues captiuity?
> Free spirits soone are caught when slaues go free:
>   What vncontrouled soule is so precise,
>   As may, yet will not tast earths paradise?
>
> *Mountioy* (the mounting ioy of heauens perfection)
> Was all a man should be in such an age,
> Nor voyd of lou's sence, nor yoakt in subiection
> of seruile passion, theame for euery stage,
> Honour for him did honours pawne ingage:

There is a notable distinction between the Earl's exalted love and the 'seruile passion' which is 'theame for euery stage': this is 1606, some twenty years before *The Broken Heart* was written: the plays of Ford's early years included, rather, *Othello* and Marston's *The Dutch Courtesan*. Yet elsewhere in the poem he shows his knowledge of the playhouse of the time, echoing *The Spanish Tragedy* and perhaps *Troilus and Cressida*. Kyd's 'O eyes, no eyes but fountains fraught with tears' was evidently in the poet's mind when he wrote:

> Life ah no life but soone extinguisht tapers?
> Tapers? no tapers but a burnt out light
> Light? ah no light but exhalations vapors
> Vapours? no vapoures but il-blinded sight?
> Sight? ah no sight but hel's eternall night?
>   Ah night no night but picture of an elfe?
>   Ah elfe? no elfe but very death it selfe.[1]

And when he claimed that Mountjoy's youthful aptitude for philosophy

> proues by instance *Aristotle* lyes,
> Who young mens aptnesse to the same denies

he is likely to have remembered Hector's words on the subject in *Troilus and Cressida*, II, ii, 165-7. We should note, however, that *Troilus* was not published till 1609. In style and quality *Fames Memoriall* shows nothing of the later Ford. But in the direction of its feeling it gives a hint of its writer's future.

So, in a different fashion, does a smaller publication of the same year. This is a prose pamphlet, justifying the ceremonial challenge of four knights on the occasion of the Danish King's visit to England. Its elaborate title was: *Honor Trivmphant. Or the Peeres Challenge, by Armes defensible, at Tilt, Turney, and Barriers. In Honor of all faire Ladies, and in defence of these foure positions following. 1. Knights in Ladies seruice haue no free will. 2. Beauty is the mainteiner of valour. 3. Faire Lady was neuer false. 4. Perfect Louers are onely*

---

[1] Four misprints are silently corrected here.

wise. Mainteined by Arguments. The young writer has plenty
of enthusiasm for his arguments, which he sets out in
affected prose, but he is clearly not taking the affair over-
seriously. He presents a gallimaufry of 'platonic love', mild
sensuality, religious doctrine, and *amour courtois*. The patrician touch appears in the assertion that '*Inconstant chaunge
beseems grosse-feeding hindes*', and there are references to
Tamburlaine and Zenocrate and, perhaps with Shakespeare's
Troilus again in mind, to Helen and Cressida. The court and
the courtly ideal were already things of fascination for him,
and there is an evident enjoyment of the literary task. He is
almost aware of the thing's absurdity, but its attraction is
stronger. His extravagances in praise of beauty provoked
someone in the early seventeenth century to write cynical
verses on female inconstancy on a blank page at the end of
the British Museum copy of the pamphlet:

> Forde can afforde much flatterring praise to women,
> wch they cannot afforde for to performe;
> perfidious are they? most vntrue to men
> farr gone in ill, and never to returne.

> Dust is lighter then a feather
> and the wynde more lighte then either
> yet a womans fickle mynde
> more lighte then feather dust or wynde

> A woman is a needfull evill
> seem

The rest is missing, as the volume has been cut: clearly 'evill'
was to rhyme with 'devill'. These are poor verses, but Ford
had given provocation enough. As we shall observe in *The
Queen* and perhaps even in *The Broken Heart*, the dramatist
might momentarily, if but half-consciously, rebel against
his own exaltation of woman's virtue and beauty[1]: in this

---

[1] See below, pp. 111-12.

early poem, however, the moment of recoil was (presumably) another's.

In many ways the strangest of all the writings associated with Ford's name was published in 1613. This was a poem called *Christes Bloodie Sweat, or the Sonne of God in his Agonie*. The title-page and the dedication give the author as 'I. F.', and Miss Sargeaunt has provided substantial reasons for identifying the initials as the dramatist's.[1] The most notable of her arguments is a close relationship between the descriptions of hell in the poem and in the Friar's words to Annabella in *'Tis Pity She's a Whore*.[2] That this intensely religious poem should thus be linked with that particular play is a hint that *'Tis Pity* is a work of unusual complexity. The dedication of *Christes Bloodie Sweat* declares the writer's purpose to show that poetry is fit for something better than '*wantonnesse*' and '*lasciuious rime*': for himself he has known '*the doubts of* folly, youth *and* opinion' and has '*long miscaried in the darknesse of vnhappinesse, both in* inuention *and* action'. The autobiographical element is also strong in the poem's beginning, when 'Gods voyce' is addressing the writer:

> Thou (quoth it) that hast spent thy best of dayes,
> In thriftlesse[3] rimes (sweete baytes to poyson Youth)
> Led with the wanton hopes of laude and praise,
> Vaine shadowes of delight seales of vntruth,
>   Now I impose new taskes vppon thy Pen,
>   to shew my sorroes to the eyes of Men.

---

[1] Sargeaunt, p. 8. Miss Sargeaunt's grounds for the attribution were first put forward in 'Writings ascribed to John Ford by Joseph Hunter in *Chorus Vatum*', *Review of English Studies*, x (April 1934), 165-76. Grosart attributed the poem to Joseph Fletcher and printed it in *The Poems of Joseph Fletcher, M.A.* (*The Fuller Worthies' Library*), 1869.

[2] See below, pp. 57-8.

[3] 'thirstlesse' 1613.

It is a long poem, running to 64 pages, and its tone is unpleasing. There is baroque imagery in plenty as the efficacy of Christ's passion is dwelt on; there is scriptural chapter and verse marginally given for many of the writer's assertions; there is fierce attack on the Church of Rome and more particularly on the Jesuits; there are repeated references to those who sinfully make a religion out of earthly love; there is one stanza that takes its imagery from the theatre:

> He di'd indeed not as an actor dies
> To die to day, and liue againe to morrow,
> In shew to please the audience, or disguise
> The idle habit of inforced sorrow:
> The Crosse his stage was, and he plaid the part
> Of one that for his friend did pawne his heart.

And there is an assertion of a Calvinistic doctrine of the elect. On this last point the writer's thought appears inconsistent, for in many places he seems to imply a general availability of salvation: nevertheless, in a passage of some length towards the end of the poem he speaks of 'soules ordain'd to Hell', of 'Egyptians' as contrasted with the chosen people. We need to remind ourselves that this poem was written some years before Ford's work as a dramatist began. We shall find religious feeling evident in *The Witch of Edmonton*, *The Lover's Melancholy* and *'Tis Pity She's a Whore*, but we shall not find it expressed in the simple and rather savage Calvinistic terms of *Christes Bloodie Sweat*. Certainly there is nothing of affectation or forced labour here. We may not like the poem, but it is as sincere as any piece of seventeenth-century puritan literature. It presents a side of Ford contrary to that shown in *Fames Memoriall* and *Honor Trivmphant*, but like them it has its notion of aristocracy. Now it is not the courtier, the devoted lover, but God's chosen who is the member of a privileged caste. And along with that there is the idea of predestination. In the

dramas of Ford one of the commonest words is 'fate', and
we have seen that suffering, not action, is the basic material
of his major plays, that the dignified acceptance of event is
the ideal he most easily offers. Indeed, the dominant figures
in Ford's plays have about them something of God's chosen
and something of the rejected: at once they form an elect,
sharply differentiated from a common humanity, and a
series of beings marked out for woe. And it requires only a
slight shifting of this viewpoint to find one's aristocracy
among the damned—a shifting exemplified by Ford in *'Tis
Pity She's a Whore*, as by Webster in *The White Devil*.
Elsewhere, however, Ford's elect are not God's enemies.

As he was to grow out of the affected language and
extravagant argument of *Honor Trivmphant*, so Ford was to
leave behind the coarseness of temper that came upon him
in the writing of *Christes Bloodie Sweat*. Nevertheless, the
poem's train of feeling was not wholly foreign to the
dramatist of later years.

Apart from a few sets of commendatory verses,[1] the only
other non-dramatic writings of Ford are two prose pamphlets in which he moralizes on the good life. The earlier,
published anonymously in 1613, was called: *The Golden
Meane. Lately written, as occasion serued, to a great Lord.
Discoursing The Noblenesse of perfect Vertue in extreames*. The
second edition (1614) made it clear that the 'great Lord' was
Henry, Earl of Northumberland, who was in the Tower
from 1605 to 1621 for alleged complicity in the Powder
Treason: in the body of the work this Earl was praised as a
type of nobility in adversity. These circumstances may
explain the anonymity of the publication. Ford's authorship,
however, is not much in doubt, for he appears to claim the
pamphlet as his in the dedication to *A Line of Life. Pointing
at the Immortality of a Vertuous Name*, which appeared in
1620. The two pamphlets are similar in tone, urging a
stoical superiority to adversity: loss of riches, exile, imprison-

[1] See Appendix A.

ment and death must each be faced with 'resolution'.[1] In *The Golden Meane* Ford again shows the patrician touch in a rejection of pity:

> It is better to be enuied than pittied: pitty proceeding out of a cold charitie towards the miserable: enuie out of a corruption of qualitie against the vertuous:

A Line of Life has a more vigorous style than the earlier pamphlet: it considers the basis of admirable conduct in men as individuals, as public figures, and in their private relations with others. The thought is unremarkable: its source is the common stock of classical precept and example, freely referred to in marginal notes, and only the occasional pious gesture is made to the Christian scheme. Perhaps it was Ford's continuing interest in the theatre that made him give Charles Duke of Biron and Sir John Van Olden Barnevelt as examples of imperfect greatness: Chapman's *The Conspiracie, and Tragedie of Charles Duke of Byron, Marshall of France* was acted and published in 1608, and *Sir John Van Olden Barnevelt* was acted in 1619[2]. In another passage there may be an echo of Chapman's *Bussy d'Ambois*. Ford writes:

> As many subtill practizers of infamie, haue other subordinate ministers of publique office and imployment in a Commonwealth, to betray them to their ruine; yet euer and anon, they like inchanted glasses, set them on fire with the false light of concealment and extenuation.

---

[1] G. C. Moore Smith, 'Anthony Stafford', *Notes and Queries*, 26 March and 2 April 1927, argued that Stafford was the author of *The Golden Meane*. The case for Ford was put by Miss Sargeaunt in 'Writings ascribed to John Ford by Joseph Hunter in *Chorus Vatum*', *Review of English Studies*, x (April 1934), 165-76. Cf. Sargeaunt, pp. 11-12. Additional evidence is provided by Davril, pp. 89-90, and Oliver, p. 18.

[2] E. K. Chambers, *The Elizabethan Stage*, 1923, i, 327.

As his subject here is the manners of those in high place, he may have had in mind Bussy's words to Monsieur concerning the court of France:

> *Mons.* . . . Leave the troubled streams,
> And live where thrivers do, at the well-head.
> *Bussy.* At the well-head? What should I do
> With that enchanted glass? (I, i.)

But Bacon had spoken of 'an enchanted glass, full of super-stition and imposture' in *The Advancement of Learning* (1605).

Though neither pamphlet is a work of distinction, *The Golden Meane* and *A Line of Life* bring to our attention an important third constituent of Ford's mentality. *Fames Memoriall* and *Honor Trivmphant* show him as the devotee of love and beauty and the court; *Christes Bloodie Sweat*, in sharp reaction, presents the Calvinist conscious of deadly sin, conscious too of a celestial prize awaiting the chosen; now these classically-minded pamphlets establish Ford's contact with Renascence stoicism. If it is *Christes Bloodie Sweat* that adds most to our understanding of *The Witch of Edmonton* and *'Tis Pity She's a Whore*, while *Fames Memoriall* and *Honor Trivmphant* illuminate *Love's Sacrifice*, it is *The Golden Meane* and *A Line of Life* that are most significant for *The Broken Heart* and *Perkin Warbeck*. That, however, is an artificial distinction, for we may find in each of his plays something of all the strains of his non-dramatic writings. And these three strains have in common the exaltation of the exceptional human being who in the depth of adversity is above the 'pitty proceeding out of a cold charitie towards the miserable'.

In 1621, the year following that in which *A Line of Life* was published, Ford collaborated with Dekker and Rowley in writing *The Witch of Edmonton*. As far as we certainly know, this was his first work for the stage.[1] It is a remarkable

[1] See Appendix A on the possibility that his dramatic career began earlier than this.

play, perhaps the best in which Dekker was ever concerned and on an altogether higher level of writing than Ford's non-dramatic pieces. As with other seventeenth-century plays written in collaboration, it is well to be cautious in assigning portions of it to one writer or another, and Miss Sargeaunt is doubtless right in her belief that Ford and Dekker in some places worked together on a single scene.[1] But the play does fall easily into three sections, and probably each of the three writers was primarily responsible for one of these. The witch of the title is Mother Sawyer, an old woman living in poverty and so often reviled as a witch that in the end she calls on the devil to come to her: he appears in the likeness of a black dog and does her bidding in wreaking a petty vengeance on her neighbours. Then he deserts her: she is taken and executed. This plot, by general agreement, is attributed to Dekker. There is a true sense of the pitiful in the presentation of the unhappy old woman, and she is given a fine eloquence when, near her end, she turns on her accusers and claims that witchcraft is a venial matter when considered along with the more flourishing vices of the world. This social criticism is indeed what we should expect from the author of *The Honest Whore*, but it is altogether remote from what we know of Ford. Plays of magic, from Greene's *Friar Bacon* and Marlowe's *Faustus*, were commonly enlivened by scenes in which the devils played tricks on low-comedy figures, and here we find that Mother Sawyer's dog amuses himself with the clown Cuddy Banks. We can safely ascribe these scenes to Rowley. The third section of the plot is the longest and the most complicated; much of it is probably by Ford, though at times he was either directly assisted by Dekker or working under a strong influence from the more experienced dramatist. The realistic presentation of a country scene and humble life seems nearer Dekker than Ford, but the writing shows an emotional intensity, a readiness to explore the mind, a

[1] Sargeaunt, pp. 37-8.

strain of religious speculation, all bearing the marks of Ford. At the beginning of the play Frank Thorney is in the service of Sir Arthur Clarington, who has seduced his maid Winnifred and then encouraged an association between her and Frank. She is pregnant, and Sir Arthur induces Frank to marry her. But he has previously been engaged to Susan, the daughter of a rich yeoman, and Frank's father is in straitened circumstances and anxious for this advantageous match. Frank has kept secret his marriage to Winnifred, and agrees to marry Susan. His plan is that he and Winnifred shall escape with the dowry. He pretends to Susan that he must go away for a time. As they are parting, the devil in the likeness of Mother Sawyer's black dog rubs against him and thus suggests the idea of murder. So he stabs Susan to death and inflicts slight wounds on himself: when he is found, he accuses two young men who have been suitors to Susan and her sister Katherine. But Frank is ill and fearful, tormented by the appearance of the black dog and Susan's ghost. Then Katherine finds out the truth when she comes on his knife still stained with Susan's blood. He repents, and is taken to execution.

A summary of the plot does little justice to Ford's share in the play. The effect is not sentimental, for the sorrows of Frank, Winnifred, Susan and Katherine are nobly borne. Frank is guilty, but his sufferings are intense. Circumstances both in Sir Arthur's household and in his own home bring him to the point where the temptation to kill Susan can become effective. There is, as we shall find in 'Tis Pity, a simultaneous presentation of the idea of fate and the idea of temptation, sin and punishment. When the devil comes to him, he has already sinned in his association with Winnifred, his bigamous marriage, and his plan to rob Susan of her dowry: he is thus, according to traditional belief, the readier to fall a prey to the greater temptation. Yet the responsibility is not all his. At the end of the play the Justice tells Sir Arthur that, though the bench hath mildly censured your errors, yet you have indeed been the instrument that wrought all their misfortunes;[1] (V, ii.)

and, like Giovanni in *'Tis Pity*, Frank is early made to cry out that his course of action is not his to choose:

> On every side I am distracted;
> Am waded deeper into mischief
> Than virtue can avoid; but on I must:
> Fate leads me; I will follow.[2] (I, ii.)

But it is important to note that at the end of this scene he links the 'destiny' of which he is aware with the moral guilt he already feels:

> No man can hide his shame from heaven that views him;
> In vain he flees whose destiny pursues him. (I, ii.)

Later he lies sick from his remorse and his self-inflicted wounds, and his thought turns to suicide. The dialogue that follows between him and Katherine shows him half-wishing that there were no world for a man to go to after death, but he has not the simple desire for annihilation that Marlowe's Faustus knew. Faustus could say:

> all beasts are happy,
> For when they die
> Their souls are soon dissolved in elements;
> But mine must live still to be plagued in hell.

---

[1] The implied comparison between Sir Arthur's and Frank's guilt is echoic of that between Mother Sawyer's and her accusers', and the touch of Dekker may perhaps be felt here.

[2] Compare:

> 'Tis not, I know,
> My lust, but 'tis my fate that leads me on.
>   (*'Tis Pity*, I, iii.)

But Frank has yet an irrepressible hope for heaven, a possibility that he cannot wish away:

> *Frank.*   Why should not I
> Go without calling?
> *Kath.*   Yes, brother, so you might,
> Were there no place to go to when you're gone
> But only this.
> *Frank.*   'Troth, sister, thou say'st true;
> For when a man has been an hundred years
> Hard travelling o'er the tottering bridge of age,
> He's not the thousand part upon his way:
> All life is but a wandering to find home;
> When we are gone, we're there. Happy were man,
> Could here his voyage end; he should not, then,
> Answer how well or ill he steer'd his soul
> By heaven's or by hell's compass; how he put in—
> Losing bless'd goodness' shore—at such a sin;
> Nor how life's dear provision he has spent,
> Nor how far he in's navigation went
> Beyond commission: this were a fine reign,
> To do ill and not hear of it again;
> Yet then were man more wretched than a beast;
> For, sister, our dead pay is sure the best.
> *Kath.* 'Tis so, the best or worst. (IV, ii.)

He has not the cold anger of Giovanni's despair: the Christian element in Frank's feeling is stronger than the sense of tragedy. Frank is to know repentance, and the prospect of salvation is with him at execution, as it was to be with Annabella when her brother plucked out her heart.

Later in this scene between Frank and Katherine there is a remarkable passage where the more tried hand of Dekker is perhaps to be seen, but its effect is so compelling that no account of the play can overlook it. Mingled here are naturalistic detail and supernatural intervention: these two strains do indeed run side by side through the play, but here their interweaving brings a special sense of conviction. Katherine, thinking that Frank has talked more than in his sickness he should, decides to bring him food: she calls out, to the maid off-stage, 'Jane, is it ready?', and the everyday enquiry arouses Frank's suspicion and fear. The raggedness of Frank's nerves is sharply presented in this fashion. Then, when the maid brings in the chicken for his meal, he suddenly feels well and ready to eat. He asks for music. On the seventeenth-century stage music was the regular prelude to a supernatural manifestation, and there is therefore a special irony that it is Frank who asks for it. Katherine arranges his pillows, so that he may eat more comfortably. He comments:

> I am up too high,
> Am I not, sister, now? (IV, ii.)

and there is again irony: he is indeed 'up too high' in the momentary confidence and euphoria that have come upon him. As Katherine takes up his vest to look for a knife, the black dog enters and dances. Frank, seeing her search and remembering the purpose for which he last used the knife, cries out that he is ill again and cannot eat. But she will be an insistent nurse: protesting that he must eat, she finds the evidence against him. Quickly she thrusts it back into the pocket, says she cannot find it, and leaves the stage. Frank himself then looks for, and finds, the knife. He says ''tis well, all's well', with the relief of despair. Then the ghost of Susan comes and looks upon him, only leaving him when the disguised Winnifred enters and stands sorrowfully at the foot of the bed. We are close here to the Elizabethan and seventeenth-century preoccupation with the death-bed.[1] All Katherine's busy and cheerful talk cannot diminish,

[1] For a useful account of this, see Beach Langston, 'Marlowe's *Faustus* and the *Ars Moriendi* Tradition', *A Tribute to George Coffin Taylor*, edited by A. Williams, 1952.

indeed accentuates, the isolation of Frank in his sickness and fear. The passage may not be Ford's, but it is one that the author of *Christes Bloodie Sweat* would understand and respond to, and we must at least remember his close association with Dekker in this play when we come to *'Tis Pity She's a Whore*.

In 1623 a play called *The Spanish Gipsy* was acted at the Phoenix theatre. It was published thirty years later, and then ascribed on its title-page to Middleton and Rowley. In recent years, however, it has come to be thought that Ford was at least a part-author.[1] The structure of the play immediately suggests a collaboration: it has two plots, each taken from one of Cervantes' *Exemplary Novels*, and linked only in the most casual way. One of them tells how the noble Alvarez was exiled for killing the father of Louis de Castro: he and his family remain in Spain disguised as gipsies, and we are shown their skill in song, dance and even impromptu play-acting. When Don John, the lover of Constanza, Alvarez' niece, is falsely accused of theft and violence, Alvarez reveals his own identity in order to save the young man. Louis de Castro is impressed by Alvarez' magnanimity and abandons his purpose of revenge. This portion of the play has a gaiety and an always pleasant humour that are unlike anything in Ford, or for that matter in Middleton or Rowley. It is nearer perhaps to the later comedies of Richard Brome, who has a talent for blending a romantic situation and setting with good-humouredly realistic dialogue and characters. In their vigorous and kindly fun these scenes may indeed remind us of Brome's *A Jovial Crew, or The Merry Beggars* (1641), where another group of people choose for a time a rambling country life. Yet there is one moment in the

[1] H. Dugdale Sykes, 'John Ford, the Author of "The Spanish Gipsy"', *Modern Language Review*, xix (January 1924), 11-24. Sykes argued for the recognition of Ford as the author of the whole play. Sargeaunt, p. 41, doubts his writing of the gipsy-scenes, and Oliver, p. 34, is not convinced that he had any large share in the play.

gipsy-plot where one might glimpse the hand of Ford. Near the end of the play it is known that Don John is a nobleman but Constanza is still believed to be a mere gipsy. Fernando assures her that there could be no binding engagement between parties so remote in rank:

> *Const.*   Will you yet
> Give me my husband's life?
> *Fer.*   Why, little one,
> He is not married to thee.
> *Const.*   In his faith
> He is; and faith and troth I hope bind faster
> Than any other ceremonies can;
> Do they not, pray, my lord?
> *Fer.*   Yes, where the parties
> Pledged are not too unequal in degree,
> As he and thou art.
> *Const.*   This is new divinity. (V, iii.)

It is not until Constanza is known to be Fernando's daughter that the betrothal is recognized. Certainly Constanza's 'This is new divinity' is a sharp reply, but the dramatist has seen to it that a misalliance is avoided. But that is a slight touch, and we must not saddle Ford with every snobbish utterance in seventeenth-century drama.[1]

It is a different matter when we turn to the more serious part of the action. That tells how Roderigo abducts Clara and rapes her. He quickly feels remorse; she tells his father of what has happened. Through his father's contrivance, Roderigo meets Clara again, does not recognize her but falls in love. They marry, and he is fully repentant and happy when all is revealed. In Cervantes' story there is a considerable time-lapse between the rape and the second meeting of Roderigo and Clara: the absence of this in the play makes the situation altogether incredible. Yet in Clara's suffering

---

[1] This part of the gipsy-plot is assigned to Ford by Davril, p. 126.

and in Roderigo's remorse there is, I think unquestionably, the accent of Ford. As in *The Witch of Edmonton*, he is concerned with sin and punishment. At one point Fernando tells his son that suffering is, and is only, heaven's vengence for sin:

> Fool, 'twere
> Impossible that justice should rain down
> In such a frightful horror without cause. (V, i.)

When Roderigo gives expression to remorse, his revulsion from sin is as strong as Frank Thorney's in *The Witch of Edmonton*:

> A thousand stings are in me: O, what vile prisons
> Make we our bodies to our immortal souls!
> Brave tenants to bad houses; 'tis a dear rent
> They pay for naughty lodging: the soul, the mistress;
> The body, the caroch that carries her;
> Sins, the swift wheels that hurry her away;
> Our will, the coachman rashly driving on,
> Till coach and carriage both are quite o'erthrown.
> My body yet 'scapes bruises; that known thief
> Is not yet called to th' bar: there's no true sense
> Of pain but what the law of conscience
> Condemns us to; I feel that. Who would lose
> A kingdom for a cottage? an estate
> Of perpetuity for a man's life
> For annuity of that life?—Pleasure!—a spark
> To those celestial fires that burn about us;
> A painted star to that bright firmament
> Of constellations which each night are set
> Lighting our way; yet thither how few get! (III, i.)

The sense that a Providence guides all is made explicit when Clara, nearer the end of the play, rejoices that 'Heaven's great hand' has 'Long since decreed' the course of events.

Though this play is agreeable in the gipsy-story and at times moving in the portion that we can assign to Ford, it is a clumsy piece of work when we compare it with its predecessor. Perhaps that was because Ford had not here the experienced Dekker to guide him. In any event, he had not yet found the type of setting or action that was to bring him to success. Neither the English countryside nor the world of Cervantes, with its diligent though sober intrigues, was right for him. He needed a less busy type of action and a setting more fanciful than the English yeoman life of *The Witch of Edmonton* or the bustling Spanish society of *The Spanish Gipsy*: only the high dignity of an imaginary court, preferably in Italy or somewhere in the eastern Mediterranean, would enable him to reach the plane of abstraction towards which his work tended. And he needed, too, the freedom of an invented story. He was to observe the working of fate in his characters, but he could feel closest to that fate, and most intimate with its victims, if he himself had contrived the manner of its working. Although in *Perkin Warbeck* he was to return to England and to the use of source-books, his general practice was to set his scene far from home and to invent actions in which the characters could display a uniformity and a distinction remote from common experience and from common imagining.[1]

[1] Though, as we shall see, Ford's independent plays make frequent echoes, in situation, character and phrase, of earlier seventeenth-century dramas, it is remarkable that his main actions seem to be almost always of his own invention. After making a diligent search for sources, Emil Koeppel reached this conclusion:

'Beim Rückblick auf die Quellenverhältnisse der Fordschen Dramen fällt uns in erste Linie auf, dass Ford, nach den bisherigen Ergebnissen der Forschung zu urteilen, die Pläne seiner Dramen häufiger als die meisten der damaligen Dramaturgen selbstständig entworfen zu haben scheint.' (*Quellen-Studien zu den Dramen George Chapman's, Philip Massinger's und John Ford's* (*Quellen und Forschungen zur Sprach- und Culturgeschichte der Germanischen Völker*, lxxxii), Strassburg 1897, p. 197.)

Subsequent research has not invalidated this. Recently R. E. Davril, 'John Ford and La Cerda's "Inés de Castro" ', *Modern Language Notes*,

But before that freedom was won Ford had made other essays in collaboration. He may have worked with Massinger and Webster on *The Fair Maid of the Inn* (1626),[1] with Fletcher on *The Laws of Candy* (*c.* 1620),[2] and perhaps with Dekker on *The Welsh Embassador* (1623).[3] He had a hand in several lost plays of this time, including *A Late Murther of the Son upon the Mother, or Keep the Widow Waking* (1624, with Webster, Dekker and Rowley), and *The Bristow Merchant* (1624, with Dekker).[4] And in 1624 he again worked with Dekker on *The Sun's Darling*, a kind of masque written for the Phoenix theatre. Possibly in this case the play was originally the work of Dekker, revised by Ford in three of its Acts.[5] It tells how Raybright, 'the sun's darling', is allowed to run through the four seasons of the year, delighting in each but quickly wanting the next. This is an allegorical picture of the life of man, in youth, manhood and old age: the sun is God, his 'darling' Raybright is man. Despite occasional bawdry, the temper is highly moral: there is an orthodox contrasting of the mutability of the seasonal year and the mind of man with the steadfastness of the cycle, the stability of the sun's order. "Tis, I see, Not in my power to alter destiny,' says Winter in Act V, and Raybright, impatient for change in the beginning, comes at

lxvi (November 1951), 64-6, has suggested that Ford took a hint from La Cerda's tragedy on Inés de Castro for the final scene in *The Broken Heart*. (Cf. Davril, pp. 176-8.) As commonly with Ford, however, the resemblance is only in an isolated dramatic situation: the plots and characters of the two plays are widely different.

[1] *The Complete Works of John Webster*, edited by F. L. Lucas, 1927, iv, 148-52; E. H. C. Oliphant, *The Plays of Beaumont and Fletcher*, 1927, pp. 463-72; Davril, pp. 140-44.

[2] E. H. C. Oliphant, *op. cit.*, pp. 472-85. Ford's hand has at times been seen also in other 'Beaumont and Fletcher' plays: see Appendix A.

[3] Oliver, pp. 34-7.

[4] On these and other lost plays associated with Ford, see Appendix A.

[5] E. K. Chambers, *The Elizabethan Stage*, iii, 299-300. The possibility that this play was a revision of Dekker's lost *Phaeton* (1598) has been weakened by the arguments of W. L. Halstead, quoted by Oliver, p. 39.

length to acknowledge the sun's wisdom. The play is on the whole gracefully done, but its generalized plan gave no opportunity for the study of an individual's being. It can, however, be linked with *The Witch of Edmonton* and *The Spanish Gipsy* in the orthodoxy of its feeling.

It is not difficult to assign more or less exact dates to these plays written in collaboration, but that cannot be said of Ford's independent plays. *The Lover's Melancholy* was licensed in 1628, *The Lady's Trial* in 1638, but we cannot be sure when the other six plays—including *'Tis Pity She's a Whore* and *The Broken Heart*—were written. It seems best, therefore, to pay little attention to chronology in the remainder of my account of Ford's development. It is likely that *'Tis Pity* was one of his earliest independent plays: it is, I have suggested, the play in which he came closest in style and thought to his major predecessors, to Shakespeare and Webster and Chapman. It is worthy of their company, and needs some extended scrutiny. I shall therefore consider it immediately after this survey of his early collaborations. Then I shall turn to those plays—*Love's Sacrifice*, *The Broken Heart* and *Perkin Warbeck*—in which Ford's special kind of tragedy came into being. Finally there will be the plays in which the ending is not tragic, in which there is usually a kindly physician to bring all things to rights. This grouping will be convenient, and perhaps only *The Lover's Melancholy* will be displaced from its chronologically correct position.[1]

[1] The early dates here suggested for *'Tis Pity She's a Whore* and *Love's Sacrifice* conflict with the view that Ford's earlier independent plays were all written for the King's men and that *c*. 1632 he made an agreement with Beeston and wrote his remaining plays for the management of the Phoenix. (Cf. G. E. Bentley, *The Jacobean and Caroline Stage*, iii (1956), 441-2.) But my basic concern is to see Ford's plays in their separate dramatic *genres*, and dating is in this a matter of secondary importance.

Ford and Jacobean Tragedy

CHAPTER TWO

FORD AND JACOBEAN TRAGEDY

I<small>F</small> *'Tis Pity She's a Whore* can be described as belonging with the Jacobean tragedies of Shakespeare, Chapman, Webster and Middleton, we must approach it by considering the attitude to the nature of things that underlies those plays. The attitude, of course, will vary to some extent from writer to writer, even from play to play—it would be absurd to equate the dominant feelings and effects of *Hamlet, Bussy d'Ambois* and *Women Beware Women*—yet it is possible to speak in general terms that have a validity for the whole body of major tragic writing in the earliest years of the seventeenth century. Basically, then, this drama is characterized by an intellectual tension. On the one side there is a feeling of exaltation in the nature of man, a delight in his dominance among created things, in his ambitions and his potentialities, his daring, his readiness to assume responsibility for the pattern of his life, his capacity for love and understanding; on the other side there is a recognition of the limitations of man's power, his isolation in the universe, the isolation among his fellows that great gifts or unusual ambition or the inheritance of high place inevitably brings, the death that must come at the end. The Elizabethans and Jacobeans were not anti-Christian when they wrote tragedy, but they were concerned with a phase of human life that began with the establishment of a perilous situation and that ended with the hero's death. They were not, during the time of composition, concerned with what might follow. At the end of *Hamlet* we have a perfunctory prayer that flights of angels will sing the Prince to his rest, and perhaps Shakespeare believed that a man who behaved as Macbeth did would go to hell. But when we see the plays we are not comforted by the thought of Hamlet among the blessed, or amended in our conduct by the thought of Macbeth's damnation. The ultimate concern in *Hamlet* is for the Prince's earthly reputation, and any celestial addition to Macbeth's sufferings, to us idle and revolting, is not explicitly affirmed in the play. In the tragedies of Chapman the indifference to the Christian scheme is more overt: for him, as for Shakespeare, there may be a world of ghosts and devils that can exercise some influence on human action, but that world is important only for its relation to the span of human life.

But, though these writers were not anti-Christian in their intent, neither were they giving us mere intellectual exercises of an 'as if' type. They were not saying, in effect, that if we were to disregard revelation this is how the world would look. Professor John Danby in his perceptive study of *Antony and Cleopatra* has indeed suggested that this was the case when Shakespeare wrote that play.[1] But *Antony and Cleopatra*, like all the major tragedies of its time, seems a much more personal thing than that interpretation would suggest. If the human situation is looked at without thought for an ultimate, supra-terrestrial setting of things to rights, it is inevitable that there should exist in the mind some feeling of resentment. This may be strong, as it surely is in Marlowe and Chapman, or subdued, as it generally appears in Shakespeare—largely perhaps because Shakespeare's interest in human characters as individuals was so strong as often to dominate his field of attention—but it is never wholly absent from Jacobean tragedy. As we see the tragic loading of the bed in *Othello* and contemplate without joy the torture which is to be Iago's, as the dead bodies of Lear and Cordelia are carried away, as Macbeth is reduced to the condition of the baited bear, we cannot feel other than at odds with the great scheme of things in which these events occur.

But resentment against the scheme of things implies a

[1] *Poets on Fortune's Hill*, 1952, pp. 149-50.

measure of anthropomorphism. That perhaps is one reason why tragedy has become increasingly difficult to write in recent years. There is something of the blasphemous in tragedy and, as G. K. Chesterton once pointed out, you have to be a believer if you are to blaspheme satisfactorily. Thomas Hardy at the end of *Tess* had to transform his Immanent Will into a President of the Immortals who was heedless and sadistic, but the last paragraph of *Tess*, eloquent as it is, does not ring true. It is too obviously a contrivance to allow for the expression of a resentment that for Hardy was irrational. But at the beginning of the seventeenth century the situation was different. The tragic writers had enough of Montaigne in them to consider the span of human life on earth as their proper study, and this concentration of interest made them uneasy and rebellious; at the same time the Christian tradition was powerful, and with part of their minds they feared God and were anxious to love him. So the continuing strength of Christian belief gave a special edge to tragic writing of that time, complicating the pride in man with a sense of guilt, leading to a strange alternation of pagan and Christian notions concerning the governance of the universe, and facilitating a convenient personalism in the apprehension of the divine. These complexities come out sharply in Webster's *The Duchess of Malfi*. The Duchess, a woman for the most part heedless of religion's claims, yet prepares herself for death with a thought of heaven and the humility needed for admission there. Yet, before she has thus achieved a mood of acceptance and submission, she has cursed the stars which she sees as emblems of the cosmic power. Bosola, her pitying tormentor, draws her attention to the ineffectiveness of such curses: 'Look you,' he says, 'the stars shine still.' She retorts that her curses have a long way to travel. Here we have an indication of the human need, very strong in the tragic dramatist, for the existence of a Being, a Power, who can feel man's resentment. Even after the Duchess has died in Christian humility (though with her last word proudly sent to her murderous brothers), the play has yet its girds at Omnipotence: it is in V, iv, that Bosola exclaims:

> We are meerly the starres tennys-balls (strooke, and banded
> Which way please them).

So, too, Shakespeare's *Lear* is full of references to the 'gods'. In his physical agony Gloucester compares them to wanton boys, later they are for him 'you ever gentle gods' as he submits to their will. They are for Edgar and Albany 'just' in their punishment of the adulterous Gloucester, the totally evil Goneril and Regan. But their justice is seen as terrible, impersonal, remote. The ultimate wisdom of Shakespeare's tragedy seems to be that our resentment should be kept in its place: love and understanding, repentance and the capacity to endure, are more important things.

If the continuing hold of a Christian cosmology gave a special edge to the tragic feeling, so did the persistence of a Christian ethical scheme. This can be seen most obviously in the complex views of revenge and ambition in the plays of the time. Revenge had always been condemned by the Church and it was manifestly, too, an offence against the social order, a usurpation of authority's privilege. But, like ambition, it gave to a man a sense of being sufficient to himself, as he assumed the right to 'Be his own carver and cut out his way'[1]: it was in tune with the Renascence pride of life, delight in individuality. Moreover, the Senecan drama gave a powerful precedent for revenge as a tragic motive and endowed the passion with classic authority. Ambition likewise was encouraged by the condition of flux in political affairs, despite its incompatibility with the traditional belief that each created thing must function within its given orbit, must not of its own will move into another. So the tragedies of the time demand our sympathy for revengers and for ambitious men. Hieronimo and Tamburlaine, Richard III

---

[1] *Richard II*, II, iii, 144.

and Marston's Antonio, Hamlet and Macbeth, Tourneur's Vindice and Webster's Vittoria, are human beings who go against the traditional injunctions: some of them are oppressed by a consciousness of the evil in their purpose, others are whole-hearted in their rebellion; but all of them win something of our esteem through their force of personality. Yet in these plays there is sometimes a hint, sometimes a manifest demonstration, that an act of revenge, or of self-aggrandizement, is evil. Kyd's Hieronimo has to pay for his revenge by his own death; Tamburlaine is stricken down at the moment of his greatest blasphemy; Marston's Antonio, having satisfied his father's ghost, enters a monastery; Richard III must experience remorse when his full course of crime is done; Hamlet must die along with Claudius; Macbeth's overthrow is an occasion for national rejoicing; the good Duke who comes to power at the end of *The Revenger's Tragedy* orders Vindice's execution; Vittoria at her death cries:

> My greatest sin lay in my blood :
> Now my blood pays for it.

Even the dramatists farthest from orthodoxy, Marlowe and Chapman, are aware of the vanity of ambition's prize, the sinking in the scale of being that revenge entails: in them there is a vein of scepticism that runs deep, but they are far from a mere overturning of Christian precepts.

In the tragedies of the time we are also made aware of the nobility of certain characters who straightforwardly exemplify the Christian virtues, from the faithful wife Olympia in *Tamburlaine* to the saintly Isabella in *The White Devil*. On the ethical plane, in fact, these plays are more confused than in their cosmology. It is a psychological commonplace that the human mind is capable of holding contrary ideas concerning the nature of a person or thing: in their cosmology the tragic writers exemplify this, never altogether parting company with the Christian scheme though presenting a picture of the world in which it is hardly manifested. But in their notion of virtue there is not so much complexity as blurring. Tamburlaine is implicitly condemned for his violence and the absurdity of his pretensions, while a minor figure like Olympia is wholly praised. Yet Marlowe can share Tamburlaine's aspirations and delight with him in his dreams of power and sensuality, at the same time honouring him for his love of Zenocrate. Shakespeare is not without a sympathetic understanding of Edmund's and Iago's egoism, he can raise awkward questions concerning Macbeth's degree of responsibility; yet there is no doubt that Cordelia, when he remembers her, is his true saint. Indeed, part of the fascination which these Jacobean tragedies hold for us lies in their shifting attitudes. We have the sense of being in a world like the one we have felt on our own pulses—where there is an uncertainty in the basis for judgment, where an ever-resurgent scepticism coexists with an inherited scheme of values. In that world the rebel can exercise a peculiar power over us, can never be quite denied our sympathy, yet can never firmly hold our approval.

But this kind of tragic writing had a comparatively short life in the seventeenth-century theatre. The major plays of Shakespeare, Chapman, Webster and Tourneur came in a very few years at the beginning of the century, and Middleton's *The Changeling* (c. 1622) has the appearance of a survival into a changed dramatic world. In general, the tragedy of the later Jacobean and the Caroline years gives us something of the impression that Professor Danby associates with *Antony and Cleopatra*,[1] an impression of a deliberate exercise in which there is only fugitive contact with the dramatist's perception of the nature of things. This mere cultivation of the dreadful, carried out with greater or less ingenuity, is illustrated at its best in Shirley's *The Cardinal*, one of the most skilful pieces of pseudo-tragedy in the Caroline theatre. Shirley knew his predecessors well and

[1] See above, p. 42.

in particular had learned much from Shakespeare and Webster: his blank verse, though it tends to diffuseness, is smooth and eloquent; his characters are conceived with an eye to a striking theatrical effect and with some psychological understanding; his plot, though it runs too easily to violence, has a continuous interest. Yet one cannot feel that this play has much existence outside the theatre for which it was written. Shirley wanted to write a successful tragedy, one that might bear comparison with earlier work, but there was no impulse in him to illustrate general fact. The usually crude statement 'He wrote from books and not from life' is applicable enough to Shirley. English tragedy, in fact, from about 1620 to the outbreak of the Civil War was, apart from Ford, to be distinguished from Fletcherian tragicomedy only in the special character of its thrill.

One cannot give a simple explanation of this change of temper in tragic writing. Partly it comes, perhaps, from the splitting of the theatrical audience into two separate sections from the second decade of the century: neither the populace of the public theatres—for which few important plays were written—nor the sophisticates of the private theatres constituted an appropriate audience for plays of great range of thought, dangerous in their implications. And a struggle was beginning in English society which was ultimately to lead to war. It was not merely a struggle between King and Parliament for political power, though indeed the very notion of such a struggle implied an oversetting of Tudor political orthodoxy. It was also, as Sir Herbert Grierson has called it, a 'metaphysical' struggle,[1] in which the forces of puritanism were establishing their hold on a great mass of the people while at court the Laudians and the Romanists found themselves speaking with similar tongues. The drama was inevitably on the side opposed to puritanism, and the intimate relations between the private theatres and the court

[1] *Metaphysical Lyrics and Poems of the Seventeenth Century: Donne to Butler,* edited by Herbert J. C. Grierson, 1921, p. lviii.

strengthened the players and the playwrights in their adherence to the court party. It is not that they write partisan or propagandist plays, as was to happen in the Restoration theatre: they are indeed quite capable of criticizing the ways of courts, of injecting into their plays sceptical utterances of all sorts. But these thrusts and moments of impatience do not become the dominating impulse in a play. The total effect of the tragedies and tragi-comedies of the time is one of a theatrical excitement which does not reverberate into the universe's dark places. Moreover, I think we must recognize in seventeenth-century English drama a simple exhaustion of the tragic spirit. Shakespeare himself did not continue to write tragedy to the end of his career. He seems to have felt a psychological need for a different approach to the world, and he found it in the final romances. These are serious plays in which the Christian ethical scheme is severely exalted, though perhaps there is rather less of Christian cosmology in them than is generally assumed. They are complicated, because they contain all sorts of echoes of the tragedies, whose world Shakespeare could not at a stroke relinquish, but they are emblematic of a striving towards simplicity, a way of looking at things that will forego at least some of the tragic antitheses. The gods are more personal now, direct manifestations of a Providence that has rewards for its own. Webster's tragedies are later than Shakespeare's, and Middleton's later still, but the tragic impulse does not remain long with either of them. By the end of James's reign the drama had ceased to make hardly endurable demands on the minds of its public.

It was in such a state of affairs that Ford set up as an independent dramatist. Earlier he had been associated with Dekker, in whose work Christian feeling is invariably strong, and Ford's own share in *The Witch of Edmonton*, *The Sun's Darling* and, we may believe, *The Spanish Gipsy* is by no means incompatible with his writing of *Christes Bloodie Sweat*. But we have noted in his non-dramatic writings a wide-spreading interest in Elizabethan and Jacobean drama: Kyd and Marlowe, Shakespeare and Chapman, all left their casual imprint on his prose and verse. He had, moreover, in *Fames Memoriall* and *Honor Trivmphant*, shown his pre-occupation with the love of woman and beauty, a pre-occupation which he perhaps over-strenuously disowned in *Christes Bloodie Sweat*:

> Loue is no god, as some of wicked times
> (Led with the dreaming dotage of their folly)
> Haue set him foorth in their lasciuious rimes,
> Bewitch'd with errors, and conceits vnholy:
> It is a raging blood affections blind,
> Which boiles both in the body and the mind.

In *Honor Trivmphant* he displayed a liking for paradox, and in *The Golden Meane* and *A Line of Life* his stoicism is pre-sented with little reference to the Christian scheme. A man in whom these contrary impulses could flourish, and who had responded freely to the tragic writing of his youth, should not surprise us if he manages to re-create in one play, perhaps the first that he wrote independently,[1] the Jacobean tragic spirit. This indeed is his achievement in *'Tis Pity She's a Whore*.

Because it is a re-creation we shall find something of strain in it. Ford goes out of his way to shock his audience. Gio-vanni must not merely rebel, as Bussy d'Ambois does: he must proclaim himself atheist. His love must be not merely illicit, but incestuous. Not only must he kill Annabella, but he must make his last entry on the stage bearing her heart on the end of his dagger. The Jacobean writers had indeed cultivated the horrible and the shocking, needing to jolt an audience accustomed to tragedy, to prevent them from merely recognizing in disaster an old dramatic acquaintance.

---

[1] The dedication describes the play as 'these first fruits of my leisure'. G. E. Bentley, *The Jacobean and Caroline Stage*, iii, 463-4, is unconvinced by this evidence, and certainly it is not to be relied on.

But there is something 'operatic', something in the Fletcherian mode, in '*Tis Pity She's a Whore*. Though when he wrote it he was around forty years of age, Ford shows something of a mere desire to make our flesh creep. That needs to be said, but the criticism does not dispose of the play. The blemish is almost inevitable when a dramatist is working in circumstances of special difficulty, is aware that his audience is hardly to be made to share his view of things. This is indeed frequent in drama, from the *Electra* of Euripides to the plays of Mr Sartre and the films of Mr Luis Buñuel.

The main action of the play concerns the love of Giovanni and Annabella, a brother and sister. In the first scene Giovanni is confessing his love to the Friar Bonaventura, who is horrified and counsels prayer and fasting. Giovanni is already in a mood to challenge the Church's teaching, yet he agrees to try what the Friar recommends. Next we meet him still consumed with passion, and he brings himself to tell Annabella of his condition. She reveals her own love for him, and for a time they live in secret joy, their relationship known only to the Friar and Annabella's gross servant Putana. Then Annabella is pregnant, and she agrees to marry her suitor Soranzo. He discovers her condition, and attempts to find out the identity of her lover. He treats her brutally, but the secret is safe with her, and she jeers at him and exults in her love—wanting to drive him to the point of killing her. Then, through a trick of Soranzo's servant Vasques, Putana is made to reveal that Giovanni is his sister's lover. Soranzo, planning revenge, invites all the city's nobles to a feast. Giovanni comes early, and Soranzo allows him to visit Annabella. The lovers realize their end must be near: Giovanni kills Annabella, and then comes among the assembly at the feast, proclaiming his love and the murder he has done, and displaying his sister's heart on his dagger. He kills Soranzo and is himself killed by a troupe of banditti whom Soranzo has hired for the achievement of his revenge.

The father of the lovers dies of grief and horror, and the Cardinal, who is conveniently present, moralizes the play's ending.

There are two subordinate actions. Soranzo has formerly seduced Hippolita, the wife of Richardetto: she tries to win the help of Vasques, Soranzo's servant, in order to revenge herself on Soranzo; Vasques, however, is loyal to his master, and Hippolita dies by her own poison. Her husband Richardetto is believed to be dead, but he returns to the city in a physician's disguise, accompanied by his niece Philotis: he too plans Soranzo's death, but this leads only to the accidental killing of the comic Bergetto, a suitor of Annabella who has transferred his affections to Philotis. I have already commented on Ford's use of crude comedy to set off the high passion of his chief characters, but the subordinate actions in this play involving Hippolita and Richardetto have an additional function. They make us recognize the moral worthlessness of Soranzo. Otherwise our sympathy might have gone to him, the convenient husband, and away from Giovanni and Annabella. As it is, we care not one jot for his deception, and our sympathy remains with the brother-and-sister lovers. This firm separation of our sympathy from Soranzo is finally ensured when, in V, iv, he permits Giovanni to visit Annabella once more, so that Giovanni may be killed fresh from the committing of sin. Those critics, incidentally, who take Hamlet literally in the prayer-scene should note the effect of this similar passage in Ford's play. Miss Sargeaunt is surely justified in her view that Maeterlinck, in his version of 'Tis Pity, was wrong to excise the Hippolita plot.[1] And, though the Bergetto affair is crude, we shall not enter fully into Ford's world unless we see his motive for introducing it, the contrast between the intensity and the reluctance of Giovanni's love and the casualness and easy pleasure of Bergetto's.

What, however, are we to make of the incest-story? In

[1] Sargeaunt, p. 108.

the opening speech of the play the Friar forbids the wanton
exploration of heaven's decrees:

> Dispute no more in this; for know, young man,
> These are no school-points; nice philosophy
> May tolerate unlikely arguments,
> But Heaven admits no jest: wits that presum'd
> On wit too much, by striving how to prove
> There was no God with foolish grounds of art,
> Discover'd first the nearest way to hell,
> And fill'd the world with devilish atheism.
> Such questions, youth, are fond: far better 'tis
> To bless the sun than reason why it shines;
> Yet He thou talk'st of is above the sun.
> No more! I may not hear it. (I, i.)

Later he admits that, were it not for revelation, there might
be something in Giovanni's claims for liberty:

> O ignorance in knowledge! Long ago,
> How often have I warn'd thee this before!
> Indeed, if we were sure there were no Deity,
> Nor Heaven nor Hell, then to be led alone
> By Nature's light—as were philosophers
> Of elder times—might instance some defence.
> But 'tis not so: then, madman, thou wilt find
> That Nature is in Heaven's positions blind. (II, v.)

This exclamation has been provoked by an argument of
Giovanni's which must remind us of Ford's theses in *Honor
Trivmphant*.[1] Here he claims that Annabella's physical beauty
implies a beauty of soul and thus a goodness in her love:

> Father, in this you are uncharitable;
> What I have done I'll prove both fit and good.
> It is a principle which you have taught,
> When I was yet your scholar, that the frame

[1] See above, p. 20.

And composition of the mind doth follow
The frame and composition of [the] body:
So, where the body's furniture is *beauty*,
The mind's must needs be *virtue*; which allow'd,
Virtue itself is reason but refin'd,
And love the quintessence of that: this proves,
My sister's beauty being rarely fair
Is rarely virtuous; chiefly in her love,
And chiefly in that love, her love to me:
If hers to me, then so is mine to her;
Since in like causes are effects alike. (II, v.)

When the lovers meet for the last time, Annabella is repentant for her sin and anxious to be reconciled to heaven, but Giovanni cannot believe in what 'the schoolmen' teach:

> *Gio.* ... The schoolmen teach that all this globe of earth
> Shall be consum'd to ashes in a minute.
>
> *Ann.* So I have read too.
>
> *Gio.* But 'twere somewhat strange
> To see the waters burn: could I believe
> This might be true, I could believe as well
> There might be hell or heaven.
>
> *Ann.* That's most certain.
>
> *Gio.* A dream, a dream! (V, v.)

Yet he attempts a compromise before the act of killing her. He hopes for her salvation and for some recognition that their incest may be distinguished from those unjustified by love:

> If ever after-times should hear
> Of our fast-knit affections, though perhaps
> The laws of conscience and of civil use
> May justly blame us, yet when they but know
> Our loves, that love will wipe away that rigour
> Which would in other incests be abhorr'd. (V, v.)

Moreover, Ford repeatedly suggests here the idea of fate, which allows Giovanni no choice but to pursue his illicit love. Thus Giovanni views his situation before he has spoken to Annabella:

> Lost! I am lost! my fates have doom'd my death:
> The more I strive, I love; the more I love,
> The less I hope: I see my ruin certain.
> What judgment or endeavours could apply
> To my incurable and restless wounds,
> I throughly have examin'd, but in vain.
> O, that it were not in religion sin
> To make our love a god, and worship it!
> I have even wearied Heaven with prayers, dried up
> The spring of my continual tears, even starv'd
> My veins with daily fasts: what wit or art
> Could counsel, I have practis'd; but, alas,
> I find all these but dreams, and old men's tales,
> To fright unsteady youth; I'm still the same:
> Or I must speak, or burst. 'Tis not, I know,
> My lust, but 'tis my fate that leads me on. (I, iii.)

Before that he has protested that he will follow the Friar's counsel of prayer and fasting, but if it fails he will know that he cannot free himself from the fate that is on him:

> All this I'll do, to free me from the rod
> Of vengeance; else I'll swear my fate's my god. (I, i.)

Yet, when the Friar tries to prevent Giovanni from attending Soranzo's feast, he defies prophecy as Bussy d'Ambois did in Chapman's play when he was warned not to go to his last assignation with his mistress:

> *Friar.* . . . Be rul'd, you shall not go.
> *Gio.*   Not go! stood Death
> Threatening his armies of confounding plagues,
> With hosts of dangers hot as blazing stars,

> I would be there: not go! yes, and resolve
> To strike as deep in slaughter as they all;
> For I will go.
>   *Friar.*   Go where thou wilt: I see
> The wildness of thy fate draws to an end,
> To a bad fearful end. (V, iii.)

This, of course, is *hubris*, but Giovanni's arrogance is at times stronger still. We hear his triumphant words as he listens in the gallery while Soranzo woos Annabella, who is not yet conscious of her pregnancy:

> *Sor.*   Have you not will to love?
> *Ann.* Not you.
> *Sor.*   Whom then?
> *Ann.*   That's as the fates infer.
> *Gio.* [*aside*]. Of those I'm regent now. (III, ii.)

And, seeing Annabella for the last time, he reproaches her for not recognizing the mastery of fate that he believes was almost his:

> Thou art a faithless sister, else thou know'st,
> Malice, or any treachery beside,
> Would stoop to my bent brows: why, I hold fate
> Clasp'd in my fist, and could command the course
> Of time's eternal motion, hadst thou been
> One thought more steady than an ebbing sea. (V, v.)

So at his last entrance he exults in his anticipation of Soranzo's revenge, his ability, as he sees it, to dominate the course of events:

> *Sor.* But where's my brother Giovanni?
>   *Enter* GIOVANNI *with a heart upon his dagger.*
>   *Gio.* Here, here, Soranzo! trimm'd in reeking blood,
> That triumphs over death, proud in the spoil
> Of love and vengeance! Fate, or all the powers
> That guide the motions of immortal souls,
> Could not prevent me. (V, vi.)

From this it is a far cry to Giovanni's earlier belief that his
guilt was not his responsibility because fate had decreed it.
Like Tamburlaine, he has come to believe, despite the
imminence of his destruction, that he holds 'the Fates bound
fast in iron chains'. His arrogance is in sharp contrast to
Annabella's passive acceptance of fate's decree as she knows
her end near:

> Thou, precious Time, that swiftly rid'st in post
> Over the world, to finish-up the race
> Of my last fate, here stay thy restless course,
> And bear to ages that are yet unborn
> A wretched, woful woman's tragedy! . . .
> O, Giovanni, that hast had the spoil
> Of thine own virtues and my modest fame,
> Would thou hadst been less subject to those stars
> That luckless reign'd at my nativity! (V, i.)

The echo of *Faustus* here[1] can hardly be accidental, and it
brings with it the notion of a terrified submission. With this
we can associate Richardetto's cry when he feels that the
dénouement is near: 'there is One Above begins to work'
(IV, ii).

There can be no doubt that in the planning of this play
Ford had *Romeo and Juliet* in mind. The Friar, Giovanni's
confidant, and Putana, the gross 'tutoress' of Annabella,
manifestly correspond to Friar Lawrence and the Nurse in
Shakespeare's tragedy of love. The point is significant, for
Shakespeare stressed that his lovers were 'star-crossed', were
not responsible for the catastrophe that awaited them. Ford,
it is evident, sees the love of Giovanni and Annabella as
an impulse that drives them to doom. Nevertheless, he
sees Giovanni's growing arrogance as at once inevitable,
splendid, and culpable.

To an early seventeenth-century tragic writer it is not
surprising that a man's conduct should simultaneously

[1] 'You stars that reigned at my nativity' (*Faustus*, V, ii).

present these different facets, and in Ford the opposition of
pagan and Christian impulses is stronger than in most.
Joined to his admiration for the adventurous Giovanni is the
stern piety that had earlier shown itself in *Christes Bloodie
Sweat*. Immediately before her marriage the Friar terrifies
Annabella with a threat of hell, and it is in this passage that
the play is closest to the poem. Here is the Friar:

Ay, you are wretched, miserably wretched,
Almost condemn'd alive. There is a place,—
List, daughter!—in a black and hollow vault,
Where day is never seen; there shines no sun,
But flaming horror of consuming fires,
A lightless sulphur, chok'd with smoky fogs
Of an infected darkness: in this place
Dwell many thousand thousand sundry sorts
Of never-dying deaths: there damnèd souls
Roar without pity; there are gluttons fed
With toads and adders; there is burning oil
Pour'd down the drunkard's throat; the usurer
Is forc'd to sup whole draughts of molten gold;
There is the murderer for ever stabb'd,
Yet can he never die; there lies the wanton
On racks of burning steel, whiles in his soul
He feels the torment of his raging lust.

   Ann. Mercy! O, mercy!

  Friar.   There stand these wretched things
Who have dream'd out whole years in lawless sheets
And secret incests, cursing one another.
Then you will wish each kiss your brother gave
Had been a dagger's point; then you shall hear
How he will cry, 'O, would my wicked sister
Had first been damn'd, when she did yield to lust!' (III, vi.)

Ford has achieved an eloquence of speech that was far
beyond him a dozen years earlier, when the poem was

written. But in devising the Friar's words he must have remembered the vision of hell that he had personally, not dramatically, represented. We cannot doubt that, when he wrote the play, the vision still had validity for him. Here is the poem's version:

> Here shall the *wantons* for a downy bed,
> Be rackt on pallets of stil-burning steele:
> Here shall the *glutton*, that hath dayly fed,
> On choice of daintie diet, hourely feele
> > Worse meat then toads, & beyond time be drencht
> > In flames of fire, that neuer shalbe quencht.
>
> Each moment shall the *killer*, be tormented
> With stabbes, that shall not so procure his death:
> The *drunkard* that would neuer be contented
> With drinking vp whole flagons at a breath,
> > Shalbe deni'd (as he with thirst is stung)
> > A drop of water for to coole his tongue.
>
> The *mony-hoording Miser* in his throat
> Shall swallow molten lead: the *spruce perfum'd*
> Shall smell most loathsome brimstone: he who wrote
> *Soule-killing rimes*, shall liuing be consum'd
> > By such a gnawing worme, that neuer dies,
> > And heare in stead of musicke hellish cries.[1]

At the end of *'Tis Pity* the situation is moralized by the Cardinal in sententious couplets, which stand in strong contrast to the last words of Giovanni, finding to the end his idea of heaven in Annabella's love:

> > > O, I bleed fast!
> Death, thou'rt a guest long look'd for; I embrace
> Thee and thy wounds: O, my last minute comes!
> Where'er I go, let me enjoy this grace,
> Freely to view my Annabella's face. (V, vi.)

[1] Two misprints are silently corrected here.

It was at this point, understandably, that Maeterlinck ended his version of the play, but to adapt Ford in this fashion is to conceal his complexity of view. He could at times see Giovanni as not merely arrogant but wholly unscrupulous in his course of evil. When wooing Annabella, he assures her:

> I have ask'd counsel of the holy church,
> Who tells me I may love you. (I, iii.)

Yet nothing that the Friar has said to him could be legitimately twisted to mean this. At this moment his wooing becomes seduction.[1] Moreover, he administers to us a subtler shock when he claims that his pleasure in lying with Annabella has in no way been diminished since her marriage:

> Busy opinion is an idle fool,
> That, as a school-rod keeps a child in awe,
> Frights th' unexperienc'd temper of the mind:
> So did it me, who, ere my precious sister
> Was married, thought all taste of love would die
> In such a contract; but I find no change
> Of pleasure in this formal law of sports.
> She is still one to me, and every kiss
> As sweet and as delicious as the first
> I reap'd, when yet the privilege of youth
> Entitled her a virgin. (V, iii.)

The passage is primarily intended to display Giovanni's condition of *hubris*, as, near the point of catastrophe, he sets himself up more arrogantly against 'Busy opinion' and rejoices in his mastery of pleasure; but also it suggests a coarsening of the character, his deterioration into an

---

[1] Oliver, p. 89, has attempted to justify his words, suggesting that 'the Friar's failure to prove a case against him is to Giovanni equivalent to condonation'. But Giovanni had surely been taught to distinguish better than this.

intriguer showing itself in his delight in the skill of his deception.[1]

Yet at the same time it is not merely Giovanni or destiny that is culpable. We have seen that the lovers hold our sympathy as no other character in the play holds it, how Ford takes pains to ensure that we shall waste no regard on Soranzo. And at one moment at least the Cardinal who moralizes the ending comes himself under a critical lash. Grimaldi has mistakenly killed the comic Bergetto and has then taken refuge with the Cardinal, who is his kinsman. When Bergetto's father Donado asks for justice, the Cardinal answers that he has received Grimaldi into the Pope's protection and will not give him up. Donado and his friend Florio protest against this ecclesiastical partiality:

> *Don.* Is this a churchman's voice? dwells justice here?
> *Flo.* Justice is fled to Heaven, and comes no nearer.
> Soranzo!—was't for him? O, impudence!
> Had he the face to speak it, and not blush?
> Come, come, Donado, there's no help in this,
> When cardinals think murder's not amiss.
> Great men may do their wills, we must obey;
> But Heaven will judge them for't another day. (III, ix.)

So we may remember this when the Cardinal takes it upon himself to re-establish the rule of law at the end of the play, condemning Putana to be burned and declaring, of Annabella, "Tis pity she's a whore."[2]

When in this way one analyses Ford's attitude to his

---

[1] This passage was a source of bewilderment to Jacques du Tillet in his review of the performance of Maeterlinck's version (*Revue Bleue*, 4ᵉ Série, ii (1894), 633-6).

[2] Mary E. Cocknower, 'John Ford' (*Seventeenth Century Studies by Members of the Graduate School, University of Cincinnati*, Princeton, 1933, pp. 211-12), has suggested that the Cardinal's prompt confiscation of 'all the gold and jewels, or whatever, . . . to the pope's proper use' (V, vi) has a satiric tinge. If so—and it seems not unlikely—this would strengthen the audience's imperfection of sympathy with the Cardinal's judgment of Annabella.

characters and their actions, one may feel only that confusion now hath made his masterpiece. But this, as we have seen, is the way of Jacobean tragedy. There is no simple faith in the man who rebels or in the law against which he rebels. There is a strong sense of sin, and of the arrogance that comes on a man as he hardens in sinning; there is a sense that he has had no choice; there is a sense that his fellows are not worthy of judging him. Above all, there is a strong sense of sympathy with the man who is apart from his fellows, making his challenge, facing his end. While we are close to Giovanni, Ford keeps us remote from the cosmic scheme, at whose nature Giovanni or the Friar or the Cardinal may only guess. There is a pattern in things, which leads Giovanni from his first impulse of love for Annabella to his murder of her and his own virtual suicide, but we have only glimpses of what that pattern signifies.

In recent years we have become used to vastly differing interpretations of Shakespeare's major plays. There is a school of critics that sees Othello as winning salvation as he dies, holding Desdemona in a last embrace; there is another school that is sure of his damnation. There are those who see the world as well lost for Antony's and Cleopatra's love, and those who are impressed by the irony of Cleopatra's sensual imaginings of a heaven where Antony is waiting for her kiss or Iras's. It is not surprising, therefore, that 'Tis Pity She's a Whore has similarly lent itself to a diversity of recent interpretation. Professor Sensabaugh sees Giovanni as Ford's sympathetic portrayal of the man who follows, and must follow, his love-impulse, being crushed by a society that will not recognize his need and the inevitability of its assertion.[1] Dr Ewing, on the other hand, is willing to dispose of the whole matter by consulting Burton's *Anatomy of Melancholy* and by diagnosing in Giovanni a religious melancholy of the atheistic kind.[2] We could not have clearer indications of the danger of interpreting seventeenth-

---

[1] Sensabaugh, pp. 171-3, 186-8.   [2] Ewing, pp. 71-6.

century tragedy either in the light of modern feeling or in the light of its contemporary psychology. According to Professor Sensabaugh,

> '*Tis Pity She's a Whore* . . . strikes the most decisive blow against the world's moral order. Here no subtle distinctions between whoredom and marriage arise; instead, the play makes an open problem of incest and thus queries the Christian idea of retributive justice.[1]

Yet we have seen that Ford, as we should indeed expect from his earlier writings, is sharply aware of sin and by no means an active unbeliever in the Christian cosmology. And Dr Ewing's simple diagnosis leaves out of account the impulse to incest that goes along with, and indeed provokes, Giovanni's religious doubts, and the reciprocal love that Annabella feels for her brother. Mr T. S. Eliot has declared Giovanni 'almost a monster of egotism' and Annabella 'virtually a moral defective'.[2] To that one might reply that, if the company of monsters of egotism is uncongenial, one had better not read much of seventeenth-century tragedy, and that a sinner who comes to recognize her guilt and to pray for pardon is a moral defective of an unusual kind. Miss Sargeaunt has rightly taken Mr Eliot to task for this exhibition of imperfect sympathy, which is doubtless due to his understandable dislike of the overt expression of moral and cosmic uncertainties. But even she falls into the irrelevant judgment, concerning this brother and sister, that Annabella is 'the better man of the two'. She praises Annabella's clear-sighted recognition of her guilt in comparison with Giovanni's 'attempts at a rational justification of their conduct'.[3] But this is to give to Ford a sureness of belief that the play hardly warrants, and it runs counter to our deep involvement with Giovanni and the strong sympathy that both he and Annabella successfully demand.

Certainly we can make a distinction between them. For

[1] Sensabaugh, p. 186. [2] *Selected Essays*, 1932, p. 198. [3] Sargeaunt, p. 186.

Giovanni we feel that 'admiration', in both senses, that normally constitutes part of our response to the Jacobean hero. Professor Davril expresses the wish that he had stabbed himself immediately after despatching his sister,[1] but this character is not one born to acquiesce: like Macbeth, like Bussy, he can take heart from a last confrontation of his enemies, and he perhaps outgoes precedent in the enjoyment of his last triumph. The conception of the hero and the violent course of action into which he enters constitute, in fact, the surest link between this play and the tragedies of Ford's predecessors, while Annabella belongs rather with the heroines of the plays that were to come. She has a close kinship with Bianca in *Love's Sacrifice*, who similarly falls into an illicit love-relationship and mocks at her husband in order to provoke her own death. And Annabella's final acquiescence in the march of events is characteristic of all Ford's heroines. She has not the strong individuality that characterizes her brother: she is nearer the dramatic symbol of error and suffering quietly borne. It is of her, not of Giovanni, that Maeterlinck speaks when, in the preface to his version of the play, he declares that Ford achieves a vision of the undifferentiated human soul:

> Ford est descendu plus avant dans les ténèbres de la vie intérieure et générale. Il est allé jusqu'aux régions où toutes les âmes commencent à se ressembler entre elles parce qu' elles n'empruntent plus que peu de choses aux circonstances, et qu'à mesure que l'on descend ou que l'on monte (c'est tout un et il ne s'agit que de dépasser le niveau de la vie aveugle et ordinaire) on s'approche de la grande source profonde, incolore, uniforme et commune de l'âme humaine.[2]

[1] Davril, p. 299.
[2] *Annabella*, pp. xii-xiii. U. M. Ellis-Fermor, *The Jacobean Drama*, 1936, p. 228, has similarly found the secret of Ford's universality 'in the knowledge of the ultimate oneness of the roots of human feeling and experience to which his concentration upon a few processes of the mind has led him'.

In conformity with this, and in contrast to her brother, Annabella has a discretion and gravity of speech, she can give a Racine-like eloquence to the simplest words:

> Brother, dear brother, know what I have been,
> And know that now there's but a dining-time
> 'Twixt us and our confusion. (V, v.)

She uses the term of family relationship, 'brother', by which she has thought of Giovanni for a longer time than their illicit love has endured; the simple reference to 'a dining-time' gives an immediacy, an association with a life we know, to her quiet and controlled speech[1]; the word 'confusion' is restrained and generalized, yet ultimate. This is the accent of Calantha in *The Broken Heart* when she recalled how 'one news straight came huddling on another Of death! and death! and death!' If we take Ford's dramas as a whole, it is his women rather than his men that remain in our minds. Giovanni, like the play he dominates, is something of a stranger in that world. But that does not diminish either his stature or that of this last, belated Jacobean tragedy.

[1] As noted in Gifford-Dyce, i, 198, there is a variant reading 'dying time'. This does, of course, make good sense, but Annabella's reference, later in the same speech, to the coming banquet as 'an harbinger of death To you and me' strengthens the case for reading 'dining-time'.

Fordian Tragedy

CHAPTER THREE

FORDIAN TRAGEDY

THE totality of human perception embraces several levels
of experience. Because, as we live from moment to
moment, we have a strong sense of the actual, of 'now', we
establish mental relationships with people, things, situations
within the shortest period of time in which it is possible to
apprehend them. We respond to, we evaluate, these objects
of our perception as if their basic character were static, not
subject to the principle of growth or to modification by
circumstance, proof against the shifting of viewpoint or
other change in ourselves. We know, of course, that this
mode of perception is partial, but we commonly act upon
it when the objects presented to our consciousness are not
such as to call memory powerfully into play. If we are
marginally aware of mutability, that may serve only to give
an emotional intensity to our response. So we may pass
judgment on a new acquaintance or a situation suddenly
encountered, or yield to the immediate charm of a landscape. If we are Romeo or Juliet, we may fall in love at a
glance. This kind of response, though normally of a lower
degree of intensity than the experience of falling in love, is
an everyday event with us. Yet, on another level of consciousness, we are aware of the world not as static but as
wholly subject to the processes of time. We trace effects
to their causes, anticipate effects from causes, finding our
patterns—pleasing or otherwise—in time rather than in
space. But this temporal mode of perception can hardly
exist without the spatial mode, which is logically anterior
to it. We cannot envisage process, mutability, without a
point of reference in an actual or imagined 'now'. We can
see this simply illustrated in Mr Aldous Huxley's recent

story, *The Genius and the Goddess*. Here the novelist's concern is predominantly with the physical and mental growth of his characters, their subjection to accident, and to some extent their cyclic fluctuations of behaviour as circumstances come near to repeating themselves. But the whole story is securely anchored in a present moment, in which one of the chief participants in the events of the story recounts it all as a remote but highly formative experience. This present moment is given elaborate description at various points in the story, and the strength of the 'now' is increased when the reader is on occasion invited to consider the likelihood of processes that are still in the future. So Proust has his 'now' from which he sets out on his search for lost time. In this way we are prevented from ever quite losing ourselves in the momentary event that occurs in the story. We know, we are perpetually reminded of, the time-pattern within which that event falls. We see the most ecstatic or dreadful moment as an abstraction from a large phase of experience. The same effect can be achieved by the taking of an already well-known story, which we shall hold in our minds as a totality while we are reading any part of it. So that, when Chaucer describes Troilus and Cressida in bed, like children together taking shelter from the rain, we are simultaneously aware of Troilus's fruitless vigil on the walls of Troy. But there too the poet gives us a 'now' as a point of reference: at the beginning of each of Books I-IV he refers to himself and his writing of the poem, so that our consciousness of time-processes co-exists with our consciousness of each apprehensible moment within the narrative.

Lessing in *The Laocoon* distinguished between painting and poetry by the assertion that the one was an art of space, the other an art of time.[1] It was, he said, the painter's concern to capture the moment as it fleeted, to seek for pattern and significance in what was offered to the senses within a period of time sufficiently short for temporal changes not to appear.

[1] Cf., especially, Chapters XVI-XVII, XX-XXI.

But the poet's concern was with processes. The painter might display Helen's beauty on his canvas, the poet should rather show men's response to it, in the launching of the thousand ships, in the old Trojans remembering their youth. In defence of his thesis, Lessing referred to the way in which memory functions. If a poet lists the various features of a landscape or a human being, his reader will not be able to bear in mind all the items in the catalogue and construct out of them an effective whole. But, while we cannot trust ourselves to memorize (and organize) a catalogue, we can simultaneously hold in the mind a series of events which are linked by a chain of causality or by any other form of consecutiveness. Because it takes time to read a poem, its material should be what happens, not what appears to have a static existence in a moment of consciousness. Now it is of course evident that those forms of art in which the mode of expression is itself subject to continuous change—the written or spoken word, music, a sequence of visual patterns—will be more easily able to objectify our sense of process, while those forms in which the mode of expression is relatively fixed—the pictorial and plastic arts—will be more at home in the field of spatial perception. Coleridge must have had this in mind when, having said that Good Sense was the body of poetic genius and Fancy its drapery, he added that Motion was its life.[1] Certainly his own poems, whether supernatural narratives or the exploration of a train of thought, are almost invariably on the move. And if Lessing is generally right in this prescription for poetry, the argument would seem to have even greater force for the drama. In the playhouse we see human beings moving before us, reacting to each other's words and actions, and composing for us an experience which continues for two or more hours. The plot, said Aristotle, is the prime element in tragedy, not the display of character or the enunciation of thought.[2] The

[1] *Biographia Literaria*, Chapter XIV.
[2] *The Poetics*, Chapter VI.

action must develop, must lead to achievement or catastrophe. If Lessing's thesis can be sustained anywhere, it is surely here.

But we must recognize that an artist is often ill-content with the limitations imposed on him by his medium. The painter, for example, will resort to various contrivances to enable himself to display his perception of process. Lessing was well aware of this, and spoke of the 'minor aggressions' ('kleinen Eingriffe') which poet and painter made on one another's rights.[1] In the Middle Ages it was possible, within the framework of a single composition, to present a series of pictures showing the same figures at different points within the course of a story. Thus the key-moments of a saint's life could be brought within a spatial relationship. Similarly, the multiple setting that was usual in medieval drama, being visible to the audience throughout the representation, would suggest a temporal coalescence of all the events in the dramatic story. Or the painter may produce a series of separate works, yet each showing an isolated step in a process. That indeed is common enough, from the traditional Stations of the Cross to Hogarth's sequences. Or, if he is anecdotally given, he may paint a single imaginary scene which immediately suggests to the viewer the events that have led up to it or will ensue. Or, with greater artists and more lasting effect, he will choose for his subject a key-moment in a well-known story: the whole action will in that way be implied.

So, too, the poet is reluctant not to make use of the momentary, spatial perception. As the painter finds himself imprisoned by his limitation to a moment of time, so the poet will feel the need to remain within that moment. He will wish to dwell on the features of a place, a person, a situation, that has confronted him within a time-unit. Though Lessing blamed him for it, Ariosto listed the charms of Alcina, and many a poet has surveyed a landscape and

[1] *The Laocoon*, Chapter XVIII.

70

drawn his reader's attention to each of its features in turn. Or he may expose different facets of a situation, as Shakespeare does in some groups of his sonnets, or as Matthew Prior in one of his songs turns from the lover to his pretended love and then to his real love and then to the invisible Venus who comments on the small spectacle they offer:

> The merchant, to secure his treasure,
>   Conveys it in a borrowed name:
> Euphelia serves to grace my measure,
>   But Chloe is my real flame.
>
> My softest verse, my darling lyre,
>   Upon Euphelia's toilet lay—
> When Chloe noted her desire
>   That I should sing, that I should play.
>
> My lyre I tune, my voice I raise,
>   But with my numbers mix my sighs;
> And whilst I sing Euphelia's praise,
>   I fix my soul on Chloe's eyes.
>
> Fair Chloe blushed: Euphelia frowned:
>   I sung, and gazed; I played, and trembled:
> And Venus to the Loves around
>   Remarked how ill we all dissembled.

It is a moment that is contemplated, and the poet isolates in turn each member of the group. However, the matter is slight and the description brief.

In the drama, though it is impossible for 'motion' to be absent, it can for a while be arrested. The most obvious illustration of this is in the Greek chorus, in those passages where neither the past is recalled nor the future anticipated but where the general significance of the play's action is expounded or where the dramatist turns away from his contemplation of a growing dread and finds relief in a lyrical reminder of natural beauty. Aristotle rebuked Euripides for allowing his chorus at times to lose contact with the dramatic action, so that a particular choral song might be as appropriate to one play as to another.[1] But in this Aristotle appears to have overlooked the dramatist's need for a point of rest, of static contemplation: to achieve this completely, it is necessary to lose contact with the dramatic action, for that cannot be contemplated without a sense of the dynamism that belongs to it. Shakespeare lacks the freedom that this use of a chorus could give: the practice of his theatre was to use a so-called chorus only for the anticipation of action or to bridge gaps in it. But he could come close to the moment of stillness in the use of the long sententious speech, where the thought is generalized, having some relation, it is true, to the action of the drama but couched in such terms that the particular application is not much in our consciousness. This is the case with Prospero's 'Our revels now are ended' and with Duke Vincentio's 'Be absolute for death'. It is almost the case, too, with the scene in *Antony and Cleopatra* where Antony's soldiers hear strange music under the stage and one of them says that this is the sign of Antony's desertion by the god Hercules: the action of the play is stilled; the god's alleged desertion is merely the symbol of a particular moment, though a decisive one, in Antony's fortunes; that moment is held, and contemplated. Thus Lessing's distinction between poetry and painting is one of emphasis and degree. Just as in our everyday experience perception cannot be wholly spatial or wholly temporal (though of course at certain times we shall tend towards one extreme or the other), so in art there is continually a reaching towards that mode of perception which the chosen art-form does not easily allow.

So far I have spoken of two modes of perception, but many people will perhaps be conscious of a third. Behind particular spatial patterns we have a sense of a general pattern which includes all particulars; behind the flux of

[1] *The Poetics*, Chapter XVIII.

things of which we are conscious through the temporal mode of perception there is a stillness which incorporates all movement, all sound. In the previous Chapter, I quoted Maeterlinck as saying that in Ford's women-characters we have an idea of the undifferentiated human soul. Individuals vary greatly from one another, but every mind knows and suffers, plans and desires, every human being is born and strives and in its fashion loves and in every fashion dies. So we are able to speak of Man, in a way that transcends mere intellectual generalization. In major works of art we are conscious of an individual person or situation being presented, but at the same time we see that the individual is humanity, the situation an image of the general human condition. Moreover, our notion of time is subsumed in a notion of simultaneity. The course of a complete action is immediately apprehensible, as it always is when we look back upon a narrative poem, a novel or a drama, which we have experienced moment by moment but which has stayed in our mind as a total image. When perception is of this order, we remain conscious of a time-sequence which is one of the dimensions of the thing we see, but we are not likely any more to think in terms of cause and effect. 'This is how it is,' we shall feel, not 'This is how it came about.' It is not that we see the different layers of time as forming an elaborate palimpsest, with the conclusion of the story as the top layer, as we do in any series of paintings on a continuous theme. Rather, we are equally aware of the beginning and of the end and of each separable moment within the sequence. In the nature of things, we shall have difficulty in achieving this kind of perception on a first reading, but a poetic dramatist, or a novelist similarly endowed, will—by means of continual echoes of preceding passages, parallels or reversals of preceding situations—urge us towards a state of mind in which we shall apprehend his work as a totality within which the separable parts, the moments of time, co-exist. In the totality of *King Lear*, Cordelia is always rejected, and Lear always in the storm, and the father and daughter always achieving peace together, and the father always holding the dead girl in his arms. In referring above to Coleridge's words on the body and drapery and life of poetry, I omitted the concluding term in his list: after assigning functions to Good Sense and Fancy and Motion, he added that Imagination was 'the Soul that is everywhere, and in each; and forms all into one graceful and intelligent whole'. A sense of wholeness is, I think, impossible if we see the arts of time as capable only of narrative, of construction within the time-dimension. When we contemplate *Lear*, we do not think of its end as the point we have to arrive at; we think of a whole in which that end is a part, as is every other moment of the play.

This has been a long but perhaps useful preamble to the discussion of Ford's three characteristic tragedies, *Love's Sacrifice*, *The Broken Heart* and *Perkin Warbeck*. They are remarkable in their comparative indifference to event, in their cultivation of the static scene, in their approach to uniformity of mood throughout the drama, and above all in their suggestion of a total vision of human life in which vicissitude has become irrelevant. From Lessing's viewpoint they are defective writings indeed, for Ford has given scant attention to the study of processes. They are, most strangely in the playhouse, analogous in effect to that Grecian urn in which Keats found only arrested movement, fairness of attitude but no imaginable end. Of course, the plays were to be acted, and they had to have plots. The characters die and sometimes kill. But a reader who makes his way through them for the sake of the dying and the killing will have little satisfaction. Defying the natural limitations of drama, Ford aims at a form of spatial perception. When we first read his plays, what remains most persistently in our minds is a series of static groupings—Penthea dead in her chair, with her brother quietly near his own end and her lover addressing words of admiration to the man he has stabbed; Orgilus,

with a proud heart, addressing himself to the formal ending
of his life; Perkin Warbeck at the moment of his entry into
the welcoming Scottish court, or later in the stocks, gracing
with little heed the confessed fraud Lambert Simnel, who
has accepted Henry's mercy and employment and now
urges Warbeck to a like humiliation; the pictures of a
solemn rite that come at the ends of *Love's Sacrifice* and *The
Broken Heart*. We shall see that he is much nearer to the
psychological drama of character and action in *Love's
Sacrifice* than in the other two tragedies, yet in all of them
the movement is towards the moment of stillness. It is no
coincidence that these most remembered moments are those
when death is imminent or just past. Here Ford, with his
urge towards a cessation of movement, is necessarily the poet
of death. The contrast thus presented between these plays
and *'Tis Pity* is extreme: there we remember with special
force the earnest colloquy of Giovanni and the Friar with
which the play opens; the fierce sensuality of the scene in
which brother and sister avow their love; the moments of
hubris and continued activity which come ever faster on
Giovanni as the end approaches; the last scene of love; and
the defiance of Giovanni's final entry.

This does not mean that the three other tragedies are mere
occasions for *tableaux vivants*, however solemn and impressive. They come, as it were, into sharp focus at such
points, but we remember them as wholes, not merely as
frameworks in which a striking picture is momentarily displayed. The death of Calantha is moving not simply because
of her firm and loving conduct in the moment itself, but
because we have seen her with other manners upon her—
listening to Penthea's account of Ithocles' love, playing the
heir-apparent, with seriousness or lightness as the occasion
demands, accepting Ithocles' love, dancing on as she learns
that all her hopes are cracked, all her loves outraged. Moreover, the plays are wholes through the coherence and con-
sistency of their language—though here indeed we must

except certain portions of *Love's Sacrifice*. Ford has his special melody in his use of blank verse, and each major character will at times give utterance to it. Poignant as his phrasing can be, there is no over-excitement of tone, no use of language for persuasion's sake—no impetus, in fact, to action. His elegiac repetitions suggest always a withdrawal into an immobility that is a refuge and a means of full realization for his characters' mode of being. 'A peine ont-ils un passé,' says Professor Davril of Ford's men and women,[1] and in effect this is true, despite the fact that in *Love's Sacrifice* and *The Broken Heart* and *The Lover's Melancholy* there is frequent reference to action before the time of the plays' beginnings: the things past are data, never strongly emphasized as causative or brought vividly before our minds. On the other hand, the frequent preoccupation with fame, chronicles, remembrance in after-times,[2] suggests the notion that the characters have within the play achieved a status beyond mutability. This is strengthened by a tendency to see them in abstract terms, which achieves its most overt expression in *The Broken Heart*. In his list of dramatis personae for that play, Ford attaches a word or phrase to each character, presenting each as it were emblematically: Ithocles is 'Honour of Loveliness', Orgilus 'Angry', Penthea 'Complaint', Calantha 'Flower of Beauty'. Some of the labels are arbitrary and almost without point, and most readers probably find the device at first sight irksome. Yet its hold on our minds is sufficient to make the characters more remote from a world of particulars, associating them and their tragedy with a plane on which abstractions can be imagined, giving to each, moreover, an immutable quality.[3]

Thus in large measure Ford compensates for his casualness of plot-development—through which he lacked some of the strongest factors making for a sense of the organic—and we are able from these plays to experience a totality in which particularities of space and time have become accidental. His

[1] Davril, p. 373.   [2] *Ibid.*, pp. 386-7.   [3] *Ibid.*, pp. 286, 432.

fascination with the spatial picture should not blind us to his deeper capacities, his perception of a poignant order of things and his manner of authority in communicating what he saw.

There is a well-known epigram by Crashaw which closely links *Love's Sacrifice* and *The Broken Heart*:

> Thou cheat'st us Ford, mak'st one seeme two by Art.
> What is *Loves Sacrifice*, but *the Broken Heart*?[1]

Certainly there is much in common to the two plays. The story of Bianca, Duchess of Pavia, who loves Fernando but determines—though without complete success—to remain faithful to her husband, has similarities to the story of Penthea, married to the elderly Bassanes but refusing to give to Orgilus, to whom she was formerly betrothed, even the hope of their marrying after Bassanes' death. In both plays, moreover, the chief woman-character dies before the end and she is much and most ceremoniously mourned. Both, as we have noted, move towards a static presentation of loss, and the dramatic incidents are casually introduced, so that we are surprised when anything happens but do not feel called on to give primary attention to the event. Incident is a mere interruption: even death is of use principally as a way of giving a final immobility to the group of figures. But the greater strength of these features in *The Broken Heart* than in *Love's Sacrifice* may indicate that *Love's Sacrifice* was written earlier. Indeed in this play there are frequent echoes both of *'Tis Pity* and of the Jacobean tragedies with which *'Tis Pity* must be associated. Towards the end of *Love's Sacrifice* the Duke returns suddenly to court, to confirm his suspicions that his friend Fernando is the Duchess's lover. He finds them indeed making love, and a scene follows in which Bianca speaks to her husband in terms of vigorous contempt, glorying in her love for Fernando. It is apparent

[1] *The Poems English Latin and Greek of Richard Crashaw*, edited by L. C. Martin, 1927, p. 181.

that she seeks a quick death and wishes to drive the Duke to the point of killing her. This is very close to the scene in *'Tis Pity* where Soranzo is brutally trying to discover from Annabella the name of her lover, and she, determined on secrecy and given over to despair, abuses him in the hope of immediate death. So too there is a resemblance in the situations of Fernando in *Love's Sacrifice* and Giovanni in *'Tis Pity*. Fernando is the Duke's friend, and finds himself loving the Duke's wife. He attempts, as Giovanni did, to subdue his love, but in II, i, he cries out in terms almost identical with Giovanni's: 'For I must speak or burst.' The play has most elaborate echoes of *Othello*, for the Duke is worked on by the villainous D'Avolos in exactly Iago's fashion. In III, ii, D'Avolos, observing Bianca and Fernando in the Duke's presence, exclaims: 'Beshrew my heart, but that's not so good', and he goes on to pretend reluctance to make himself plain. The Duke turns on him in the following scene, his threats owing much to Othello's:

> Thou art a traitor: do not think the gloss
> Of smooth evasion, by your cunning jests
> And coinage of your politician's brain,
> Shall jig me off; I'll know 't, I vow I will.
> Did not I note your dark abrupted ends
> Of words half-spoke? your 'wells, if all were known'?
> Your short 'I like not that'? your girds and 'buts'?
> Yes, sir, I did; such broken language argues
> More matter than your subtlety shall hide:
> Tell me, what is't? by honour's self I'll know. (III, iii.)

In IV, i, D'Avolos has grown bolder and urges upon the Duke an imaginary picture of the two lovers as they 'exchange kisses, seeking one another's lips, nay, begetting an heir to the dukedom, or practising more than the very act of adultery itself'. When in the last Act the Duke has come to believe Bianca innocent, he expresses his despair, his inability to envisage life on any terms, in words that recall

Othello's remorse and his terror at the thought of Desdemona's reproachful presence at the judgment seat. And he
sees D'Avolos as the devil that Othello came to see in Iago:

> Slave, torture me no more!—Note him, my lords;
> If you would choose a devil in the shape
> Of man, an arch-arch-devil, there stands one. (V, ii.)

Ford was so preoccupied with *Othello* here that he even gave
Fernando a soliloquy reminiscent of Iago's. Love has just
taken possession of him, and he debates its claims and those
of friendship, the chance of success with Bianca, and the
means of revealing his passion to her, in a way strongly
echoic of Iago's early deliberations, staccato, colloquial, with
all the marks of active and fevered thought:

> So, now I am alone; now let me think.
> She is the duchess; say she be; a creature
> Sew'd-up in painted cloth might so be styl'd;
> That's but a name: she's married too; she is,
> And therefore better might distinguish love:
> She's young and fair; why, madam, that's the bait
> Invites me more to hope: she's the duke's wife;
> Who knows not this?—she's bosom'd to my friend;
> There, there, I am quite lost: will not be won;
> Still worse and worse: abhors to hear me speak;
> Eternal mischief! I must urge no more;
> For, were I not be-leper'd in my soul,
> Here were enough to quench the flames of hell.
> What then? pish! [if] I must not speak, I'll write. (II, ii.)

And there are echoes of Webster too in the play. The first
words of the first Act are Roseilli's 'Depart the court?',
which is close to Lodovico's angry cry 'Banished!' at the
beginning of *The White Devil*. A minor villain Ferentes
takes his leave with an utterance close to Vittoria's in
Webster's play[1]: 'My forfeit was in my blood; and my life

[1] See above, p. 45.

hath answered it.' And when the Duke's sister Fiormonda is wooing Fernando for herself, she produces a ring that her first husband had given her and tries to persuade Fernando to take it—all very much in the manner of the Duchess of Malfi wooing her steward Antonio.

Yet these echoes of *'Tis Pity* and of Shakespeare and Webster do not give to *Love's Sacrifice* its characteristic quality. That, rather, is one of lamentation for ineluctable distress. The fourth Act ends with an emphasis on the working of fate, as Roseilli says of Fernando:

> I see him lost already.
> If all prevail not, we shall know too late
> No toil can shun the violence of fate. (IV, ii.)

We are, in fact, made to feel that the love-relationship of Bianca and Fernando is an inevitable consequence of their situation. She, young and dowerless, has married the elderly Duke: Fernando is his young friend, and Bianca is fair: she resists his wooing, thinking to bring the matter effectively to a stop by going to him at night and offering to accept his love, while making it plain that, if he allows her to do this, she will kill herself in the morning. Fernando, of course, responds generously and abandons for a while any thought of her love. Then Ford's shrewdness of understanding is shown most finely. Bianca becomes increasingly imprudent, increasingly a prey to the love that she has apparently succeeded in bringing to an end. In III, ii, she and Fernando are on stage with the Duke and his courtiers. She speaks, apart, to Fernando, asking him: 'Speak, shall I steal a kiss? believe me, my lord, I long.' The previous assertion of her virtue has so satisfied her scruples that now she is heartily ready to accept Fernando's love, and will show her feelings with folly and rashness. After she has driven the Duke to kill her, we are again made to feel the inevitability of his new belief in her innocence: he has been too devoted to the idea of her to be able indefinitely to think her disloyal. So he and

Fernando join in doing her posthumous honour, and together they kill themselves to escape from their sense of loss.
We are left with an image of these three people and their
relationships: there is no question of blame, or of praise;
but there is much pity, and Ford joins the two men in their
devotion to Bianca.[1]

It will be seen that the main plot of *Love's Sacrifice* is of
the slightest. Ford filled out his play with various court-
intrigues, to some degree incorporating the dully farcical
comedy which was so often a blemish on his work. He was
to do better than this in *The Broken Heart*, where he secured
enough material for his five Acts by a skilful interweaving
of actions, all of which, however, had the high seriousness
that his tragedy needed. *Love's Sacrifice* thus has all the marks
of being an intermediary play between *'Tis Pity* on the one
hand and *The Broken Heart* and *Perkin Warbeck* on the other.
Nevertheless, it is to be valued for its central action involving
Bianca, who has been drawn by Ford with a supreme
understanding of human waywardness and a woman's
passion.

If Professor Alfred Harbage is right in his belief that *The
Great Favourite, or The Duke of Lerma*, published as the work
of Sir Robert Howard in 1668, is an adaptation of a lost play
by Ford,[2] it is probable that in the original form it had a
strong family likeness to *Love's Sacrifice*. In Howard's
version it shows how the Duke of Lerma re-establishes his
tottering fortunes by loosing his daughter Maria to the
young King of Spain: she is virtuous, but when the King

---

[1] The final homage offered to Bianca makes it difficult to accept the
argument of Peter Ure ('Cult and Initiates in Ford's *Love's Sacrifice*',
Modern Language Quarterly, xi (September 1950), 298-306) that Fernando
is an 'idealistic practitioner of the closely related ethics of friendship
and Platonic love', while Bianca is 'not a true initiate of the Platonic
cult'. Moreover, Fernando, in his soliloquy in II, ii, quoted above,
does not seem Platonically given and recognizes the claims of friendship only to dismiss them.

[2] See Appendix A, p. 130.

falls quickly in love with her there is a general assumption in the court that she is his mistress. She wishes to save her father from ruin, but will not sell her love or approve of his unscrupulous dealing with his enemies. The King and court are ultimately convinced of her virtue. Her father saves himself from the growing power of his rivals by purchasing a Cardinal's office: he has a splendid last entrance when he confronts his judges in his Cardinal's robes, and Howard's preface indicates that this was in the 'old play' he had adapted. It is, of course, impossible to say how much of the extant version is Ford's, but we can surely detect Howard in the very ending of the play: this is largely in couplets, and shows Maria slowly yielding to the King's wish to make her his Queen. In his preface, Howard says of the original:

> it ended abruptly: and on the person of Philip the 3 there was fixed such a mean character, and on the daughter of the Duke of Lerma such a vicious one, that I could not but judge it unfit to be presented by any that had a respect, not only to princes, but indeed to either man or woman.

In Howard's version Maria has no trace of viciousness. She is as virtuous and as calumniated as Spinella in *The Lady's Trial*, and like Spinella she disappears from view during the later part of the play, returning at the end for a solemn exculpation. But the 'old play' made her 'vicious', and we must therefore assume that her character was there nearer Bianca's than Spinella's. Professor Harbage has wondered if Ford suggested an incestuous relationship with her father, for certainly Lerma often describes her with an unusual fervour. This possibility is strengthened when we consider than an incest-motive shows itself in *The Broken Heart* as well as in *'Tis Pity*. But it is unlikely that it was the mainspring of the action. The whole conduct of the plot depends on Lerma's use of his daughter to re-establish himself as the King's favourite, and on her reluctance to play her part. Though it is rash to speculate on the exact sequence of events in the 'old play', it seems possible that Ford's Maria was rather more wavering in her virtue than Howard's, that like Bianca's her resistance to the power of love was not lasting, that Lerma's fall was ultimately bound up with the King's view that a mistress, once attained, was but a mistress. In IV. i, her uncle the Duke of Medina comes in disguise to Maria and presents a masque-like entertainment which is intended to arouse the workings of her conscience: she protests her virtue indignantly and nobly, so that Medina is astonished and begins to wonder if calumny has been done. It would be close indeed to *Love's Sacrifice* if her yielding to the King had quickly followed this successful demonstration of her virtue. Howard said the King's character was 'mean' in the original, and we can have no doubt that, as in *Love's Sacrifice* and *The Broken Heart*, Ford would here have put all his strength and admiration at Maria's disposal. There would, however, be no opportunity for a last-act glorification of his heroine. Howard, we have seen, said the old play 'ended abruptly', and Lerma's triumphant withdrawal from his judges and the world, safe in his Cardinal's scarlet, was doubtless almost the last incident. There would be no final entry for Maria, no elevation to a throne. There is no historical warrant for Maria's existence, but the real Duke of Lerma had a son who turned against him, and Philip IV— the successor of the King in the play—had a mistress called Maria Calderon.[1] Ford's Maria may well have been nearer than Howard's to the historical Duke's son and King's mistress.

In Howard's version Lerma is presented as a man ready to challenge fate:

> *Mar.* Are there divinities below?
> *Ler.* There are. Every wise thing is a divinity
> That can dispose and check the fate of things. (II, i.)

[1] *Dryden & Howard 1664-1668*, edited by D. D. Arundell, 1929, pp. 209-10.

But his efforts are puny: he cannot control Maria's will, his hold on the King is always insecure, his enemies are finally able to drive him from court. When the play ends, his one remaining achievement is a purchased immunity from death and imprisonment, and it seems a small matter for one who sought 'divinity'. Maria, on the other hand, though he would use her as an instrument in his advancement, has always his homage and the King's. It is her initial bewilderment, her love for the King which yet will not kill her virtue, her resolution in defying the King's lust, curbing her father's plans and yet seeking to preserve him, that provide the play with its centre. The scenes in which she meets her father or the unprincipled Confessor or the King or her uncle Medina have Ford's note in them. And if we have lost a later scene between her and the King, we have lost the chance of seeing her as vividly as we see Bianca. Nevertheless, the play may have been left unpublished by Ford because he could not devise an ending satisfactory to him.[1]

The action of *The Broken Heart*, like that of *'Tis Pity She's a Whore*, is centred in a brother and a sister, Ithocles and Penthea. Indeed at one point in the play Bassanes, the husband of Penthea, suspects that she and Ithocles are lovers. And at another point we are reminded of the earlier play when Orgilus manifestly resents his sister's acceptance of Prophilus's love. These, however, are only stray echoes: as in *Love's Sacrifice*, the stress here is on suffering, not on the daring and violence of Giovanni and Annabella. Penthea, we learn, was formerly betrothed to Orgilus, but Ithocles was ambitious and contrived for her the more splendid match with Bassanes. She and Orgilus suffer from their

[1] Recently doubt has been thrown on the ascription to Ford (Oliver, pp. 131-9). Certainly we should not regard the problem of authorship as settled, but the presentation of Maria, and the hints given by Howard as to her character in the 'old play', may still incline us to accept Professor Harbage's view.

separation, and there is a touch characteristic of Ford when she tells him that, even after Bassanes' death, she will not allow Orgilus to take her at second-hand:

> *Org.* . . . Penthea is the wife to Orgilus,
> And ever shall be.
> *Pen.*   Never shall or will.
> *Org.* How!
> *Pen.*   Hear me; in a word I'll tell thee why.
> The virgin-dowry which my birth bestow'd
> Is ravish'd by another; my true love
> Abhors to think that Orgilus deserv'd
> No better favours than a second bed.
> *Org.* I must not take this reason.
> *Pen.*   To confirm it;
> Should I outlive my bondage, let me meet
> Another worse than this and less desir'd,
> If, of all men alive, thou shouldst but touch
> My lip or hand again! (II, iii.)

This is one of the most unpleasant manifestations of Ford's exaltation of beauty and virginity, a peculiar exhibition of a snobbery that disregards the person while exalting its condition. One would be willing to believe that here Ford has insight into the quirks that may afflict a human being in a state of deprivation, but Penthea is so generally exalted in the play that this seems unlikely. While Penthea, however, is thus morbidly faithful, Bassanes is jealous, and Penthea is ultimately driven to a state of mind in which she starves herself to death. Ithocles has long repented his arrangement of his sister's marriage, and recognizes the wrong he has done to her and Orgilus. Penthea forgives him, and pleads on his behalf to Calantha, the Princess of Sparta, whom he loves. Orgilus respects Ithocles, but cannot allow him to escape unpunished. In the presence of Penthea's dead body, he kills Ithocles, admiring his fortitude and being ready himself to die for what he has done. At Calantha's order he gives

himself to death, with resolution, no thought of a compen-
sating heaven, no remorse:

> *Org.*   I feel no palsies.
> On a pair-royal do I wait in death;
> My sovereign, as his liegeman; on my mistress,
> As a devoted servant; and on Ithocles,
> As if no brave, yet no unworthy enemy:
> Nor did I use an engine to entrap
> His life, out of a slavish fear to combat
> Youth, strength, or cunning; but for that I durst not
> Engage the goodness of a cause on fortune,
> By which his name might have outfac'd my vengeance.
> O, Tecnicus, inspir'd with Phoebus' fire!
> I call to mind thy augury, 'twas perfect;
> *Revenge proves its own executioner.*
> When feeble man is bending to his mother,
> The dust he was first fram'd on, thus he totters.
>   *Bass.* Life's fountain is dried up.
>   *Org.*   So falls the standard
> Of my prerogative in being a creature!
> A mist hangs o'er mine eyes, the sun's bright splendour
> Is clouded in an everlasting shadow;
> Welcome, thou ice, that sitt'st about my heart,
> No heat can ever thaw thee.   [*Dies.*
>   *Near.*   Speech hath left him.
>   *Bass.* He has shook hands with time. (V, ii.)

Calantha, too, as we saw earlier, goes to her death with
dignity as well as with a broken heart.

If we were to seek for the beginning of the series of
disasters that the play exhibits, we should find it in Ithocles'
arranging of his sister's marriage to Bassanes. But that seems
irrelevant to the play's effect. There is hardly a character
here that does not demand our sympathy: Ithocles, truly
repentant of the wrong he has done his sister; Penthea,

suffering from Bassanes' jealousy and from her reciprocated love for Orgilus; Orgilus, with malice towards none but with a sense of compulsion to kill Ithocles for his responsibility for Penthea's death; Bassanes, absurdly, pathologically jealous, but pathetically so, and at the end of the play rousing his strength so that jealousy may be overcome, sorrow endured, and respects rightly paid; Calantha, ever the Princess yet a woman in love with Ithocles and a devoted subject of death when her lover has entered its dominion. These characters win our sympathy, not for what they do, but for their readiness to suffer their fate with a measure of dignity. It is not surprising, therefore, that the dialogue of the play is full of references to fate. Tecnicus, the tutor of Orgilus, thus teaches resignation to his pupil:

> Tempt not the stars; young man, thou canst not play
> With the severity of fate. (I, iii.)

So Prophilus, the lover of Orgilus's sister, says: 'Fate instructs me' (I, ii), and Calantha is described as 'cross'd by fate' (IV, iii). Ithocles thus submits himself:

> Leave to the powers
> Above us the effects of their decrees;
> My burthen lies within me: servile fears
> Prevent no great effects. (IV, i.)

And Nearchus, the Prince of Argos who succeeds to the kingship of Sparta on Calantha's death, asserts man's ignorance of heaven's decree:

> The counsels of the gods are never known
> Till men can call th' effects of them their own. (V, iii.)

This contrast between the ordaining gods and their puppets men is expressed too by Orgilus:

> Mortality
> Creeps on the dung of earth, and cannot reach
> The riddles which are purpos'd by the gods. (I, iii.)

And by Tecnicus when he says:

> But let the gods be moderators still;
> No human power can prevent their will. (III, i.)

In Jacobean tragedy there was a simple opposition implied between the vigour and daring of human beings and the fixed character of divine decree. Here the characters are not vigorous: certainly Ithocles has been the successful commander of an army, and Orgilus has the degree of resolution requisite for the killing of his friend, but it is not their daring but their courtly dignity that makes itself most apparent to us. Penthea, Ithocles, Orgilus, Calantha do not protest against the manner or the early coming of their deaths. They are far more preoccupied with the need to go out well. Ithocles dreams of a heaven awaiting him:

> Thoughts of ambition, or delicious banquet
> With beauty, youth, and love, together perish
> In my last breath, which on the sacred altar
> Of a long-look'd-for peace—now—moves—to heaven.
>
> (IV, iv.)

But the other characters have their minds elsewhere, on love and deprivation and the need to leave a kingdom in good order, a sovereign's name in good repair. Perhaps Ford considered that Ithocles, sympathetic character as he was, had done most wrong in frustrating the love of Penthea and Orgilus: consequently he needed a thought of heaven to make quiet the anguish of his remorse, while the others, even the murderer Orgilus, could go into darkness with only a need for 'resolution'. With all, however, there is a sense that they are most supremely themselves in the moment of death, that this moment definitively marks their characters, makes them proof against mutability.

As usually with Ford, there are clumsinesses in the contrivance of the action. He seems to forget details that he had at first meant to seem important.[1] Thus in I, iii, Orgilus is disguised, and his sister Euphranea and her lover Prophilus plan to use him as a means of writing to each other. This is ironic, for Orgilus is jealously opposed to the match. But the whole device is quickly forgotten, and Orgilus abandons his disguise and returns to court. So in IV, iii, Ithocles tells Orgilus of his still hopeless love for Calantha, though the King's consent to the marriage had been made public shortly before. And, though the effect in V, ii, is admirable, when a series of messengers brings to the dancing Calantha the news that her father and Penthea and Ithocles are dead, we may well feel incredulous that she should be informed in this stylized way: the dramatic method employed in the scene does not quite cohere with the general manner of the play. As ever, we feel that Ford is not to be bothered with matters of detail. There are, of course, other things that stand in a modern reader's way when he would enter sympathetically into the world of *The Broken Heart*. He may find Penthea morbid in her cult of virginity, when she will not consider offering to Orgilus the blown flower of her widowhood, and he may resent the snobbishness of Calantha as, at the moment of her death, she contrasts herself to 'mere women' who may outlive their sorrows. It is even possible that Ford's preoccupation with sexual love may seem too exclusive.

Nevertheless, the play presents an imaginable world consistently peopled, and its inhabitants speak in fittingly noble accents. And our admiration for them is made sharper because we feel that some effort has gone into the act of

[1] Emil Koeppel was perhaps right in his belief that Ford originally intended a love-affair between Ithocles and Euphranea, the sister of Orgilus: this would explain Orgilus's extraction of a vow from Euphranea in I, ii, that she will not marry without his consent (*Quellen-Studien zu den Dramen George Chapman's, Philip Massinger's und John Ford's*, pp. 177-8). It seems more likely, however, that this incident and Orgilus's later reluctance to agree to Euphranea's marriage with Prophilus merely indicate his possessive disposition, manifested at its height in his relations with Penthea.

imagining. Ford is not at every moment sure that this aristocratic world is wholly firm or admirable: he makes Orgilus protest against the King's arbitrary order for the marriage of Euphranea and Prophilus; he makes Ithocles behave churlishly to the Prince of Argos when he thinks that Calantha will accept the Prince's alliance; and the near-madness of the jealous Bassanes, the suspicion of incest that comes to him, and the over-possessive attitude of Orgilus to his sister, are forces that could disrupt this well-conducted school of suffering. So, in imagining the 'Sparta' that is this play's nominal scene, Ford is expressing a wish for a proud and yet affectionate courtliness which he cannot fully credit. It is this hint of an ultimate uncertainty, a fragility in the structure of his palace of art, that makes us doubtful of Professor Ellis-Fermor's view of his plays: she sees Ford as approaching suffering and abnormality 'with a grave and unfaltering faith in the ultimate prevalence of underlying virtue in the universe of mind', and in his plays, she suggests, 'we assist . . . at the conversion of the seven deadly sins, not at their overthrow'.[1] It would certainly be difficult to see this as true of 'Tis Pity, where Giovanni's defiance and guilt remain with him to the end. And in The Broken Heart the assertion of human nobility has the hint of precariousness that strengthens our aspiration, that makes us strive towards belief. For the dream, however nearly at times the poet comes to the point of waking, is superbly managed. It is not 'life' as we know it: yet it is an aspiration that we certainly know, a condition in which human beings might behave as Ithocles and Calantha and Penthea do. It is, if one likes to phrase it so, a kind of sainthood that the poet here formulates and loves. And the saints have respect and affection for one another. Ithocles mourns for the loss of Penthea's happiness and worships her in her death; Orgilus kills Ithocles with words of deep admiration on his lips; Calantha condemns Orgilus to death, but, though he has killed her love, with a

[1] *The Jacobean Drama*, pp. 245-6.

tender sorrow; Bassanes, recovered at last from his fears of cuckoldom, pays a deep respect to his wife, her brother, her lover and the Princess Calantha who dies last of all. Bassanes, indeed, was earlier in the play so full of jealous anger that, as we have seen, he sounded a dangerous note in the quiet sadness of this dramatic world. But at its end he too is quiet, he has come over to the quietist ideal: he has learned the dignity of not coveting, of being ready to lose all, of a nobleness which is self-conscious and ultimately sufficient.

It is natural that to-day these figures should associate themselves in our minds with the joint protagonists of Villiers de l'Isle-Adam's *Axël*, and indeed Mr Camille Cé has made this association explicit.[1] But Axël and Sara not only challenge the worlds from which they have come but of their own will choose to give up a life that is beneath their regard: 'Vivre? les serviteurs feront cela pour nous.' It is this challenge and this contempt for mere being that differentiate them from Ford's characters. Penthea and Orgilus, Calantha and Ithocles, do not revolt against their Sparta and its ways, they do not seek destruction: they merely and grandly submit when nature or the law or emotional exhaustion demands their ending. As symbols they have not the power to startle that belongs securely to Axël and Sara. It is in a gentler fashion that they make their claims on us; it is a more orthodox cosmology that they inhabit; it is, ultimately, a less 'romantic' impulse that has gone to their making.

To-day we could not expect *The Broken Heart* to be a popular tragedy. We have to make an effort of the historical imagination to come to terms with it. Yet, when we have done so, we not merely understand more of the special nature of English drama in Charles I's reign: we are more deeply aware of a special kind of human aspiration, the desire not merely to 'get on', to win applause for achievement, to satisfy one's sensual or other material longings, but

[1] Quoted by Davril, p. 497.

to accept the inevitable with calm and authority. And that, after all, is not the most contemptible of aspirations.

In *Perkin Warbeck* Ford turns from the nobility to an impostor. Professor Lawrence Babb has pointed out that, although the chroniclers presented him 'as an impudent rascal who is under no illusions regarding his base origin', Ford never questions his sincerity. In the play he is a melancholic who has come to believe in his own royalty.[1] To us his pretensions are exposed by means of the tag-rag company who are his only persistent followers, and through the blunt scepticism of the Earl of Huntley. But it was doubtless Warbeck's final refusal to come to terms with Henry, knowing that his refusal meant death, that attracted Ford to his story. Warbeck becomes a Fordian aristocrat, dignified by his own steadfastness in delusion. Moreover, though Professor Babb's diagnosis compels itself on us through Warbeck's dramatic situation, Ford never exposes him to the pity which we may give to the sick. That he speaks like one sure of himself, not like one deranged, has made Professor Davril refuse to see him as afflicted,[2] and we may say that Ford has here achieved probability in character and action by a most discreet employment of the knowledge he derived from Burton. To act as he does, Warbeck must be afflicted, yet nothing in his own words or in the attitude of the other characters confirms this necessary view of his condition. For a time he can win the support of the King of Scotland, and more abidingly the love of Lady Katherine Gordon. Indeed Ford departs from his sources when he tells us that Katherine will 'die a faithful widow', overlooking her historically subsequent marriages in order to make her a more zealously Fordian heroine and to make of Warbeck a man more clearly distinguished in the love he could inspire.

The play is very different from the chronicle histories of

[1] 'Abnormal Psychology in John Ford's *Perkin Warbeck*', *Modern Language Notes*, li (April 1936), 234-7.
[2] Davril, pp. 228-9.

thirty or forty years earlier. Here we have little in the way of fighting or pageantry. The interest is on Warbeck and Lady Katherine and her true, respectful lover Lord Dalyell, and to some extent on Henry VII, a man crafty in the political struggle yet truly perturbed by the malignancy of those about him. When, at the beginning of the play, Henry is told that his friend Sir William Stanley is plotting against him, the King's grief is extreme. He has not the controlled indignation that Shakespeare made Henry V show at South-ampton: he is wounded deeply, and laments the loss of a good man. Certainly Ford remembers the earlier histories a little, and perhaps because of that he makes reference to kingship's divinity:

> But kings are earthly gods, there is no meddling
> With their anointed bodies; for their actions
> They only are accountable to heaven. (III, ii.)

Warbeck, ever secure in his own delusion, makes a similar assertion:

> Herein stand the odds,
> Subjects are men on earth, kings men and gods. (IV, v.)[1]

But what emerges as of most importance here is not kingly birth or position but the belief, however won, in one's own aristocracy, in the unwavering acceptance of the role of greatness. In this play modern readers may feel that Ford's notion of aristocracy has been modified. Perhaps indeed it has, yet it is still based on a qualitative discrimination be-tween high and low. Warbeck, in aspiring to recognition as

[1] M. C. Struble, in her edition of the play (*University of Washington Publications in Language and Literature*, iii, Seattle 1926, pp. 30-37), suggests that Ford was tactfully displaying in *Perkin Warbeck* a Tudor rather than a Stuart notion of monarchy, with a hint of a social contract and royal responsibility. But this is to read too much into some casual utterances in the play. In any event, Ford's dominant concern was, as ever, with his chosen human figures.

a king, has assumed and accepted the responsibilities that belong to the high: it is to his honour that his conduct befits his claim, but it is the aspiration to high rank that brings a chance of distinction to him. Early in the play Sir Robert Clifford has betrayed Sir William Stanley's share in a plot against the King: Stanley asks to see Clifford before he dies: when he comes, Stanley marks his cheeks with a cross, as a badge of infamy:

> I wet upon your cheeks a holy sign,—
> The cross, the Christian's badge, the traitor's infamy:
> Wear, Clifford, to thy grave this painted emblem;
> Water shall never wash it off; all eyes
> That gaze upon thy face shall read there written
> A state-informer's character; more ugly
> Stamp'd on a noble name than on a base. (II, ii.)

The aristocratic touch is obvious enough here: the informer's mark is 'more ugly Stamp'd on a noble name than on a base': Sir Robert Clifford, playing the political opportunist, has betrayed the rank in which he was born. This play is not about a struggle for power, as for the most part the histories of the 1590s had been. It is, like *The Broken Heart* and to some extent *Love's Sacrifice*, a demonstration of how nobility can be rightly worn. Thus Warbeck's disreputable companions, though their comedy is ineptly written, have a dramatic function in their contrast to their leader; and there is an occasional hint of a contrast between the capable and crafty king, Henry VII, and the noble and unpractical impostor, Warbeck.

The play is as full of references to fate as the other tragedies of Ford, and once again we are made more fully aware of human powers as their limitations are exposed. Frion, Warbeck's secretary and the only man of intelligence among his followers, sees that the issue of the strife with King Henry is determined in advance:

> yet our tide
> Runs smoothly, without adverse winds: run on!
> Flow to a full sea! time alone debates
> Quarrels forewritten in the book of fates. (II, iii.)

So Katherine exhorts her husband to accept whatever is bound to come:

> What our destinies
> Have rul'd-out in their books we must not search,
> But kneel to. (III, ii.)

But Warbeck needs little urging to this, as he proclaims his readiness to follow the line of event that he does not claim to control:

> Be men, my friends, and let our cousin-king
> See how we follow fate as willingly
> As malice follows us. (IV, iii.)

When disaster comes, Katherine can find a value in the immutability of fate, which can test her ability to meet it:

> It is decreed; and we must yield to fate,
> Whose angry justice, though it threaten ruin,
> Contempt, and poverty, is all but trial
> Of a weak woman's constancy in suffering. (V, i.)

Here Ford is close to Webster, whose choric character Delio in *The Duchess of Malfi* exclaims:

> Though in our miseries Fortune have a part,
> Yet in our noble suff'rings she hath none.
> Contempt of pain, that we may call our own. (V, iii.)

But neither in *Perkin Warbeck* nor in his other tragedies does Ford give us the impression that his characters are stretched and tormented as Webster's are. Rather, it is of the nature of

Ford's elect that they endure their trials (which are poignant but never savage) with a calm readiness. Webster's, on the other hand, have no natural inclination to passivity: they are full of passion and initiative, achieving a final acceptance at the cost of a supreme effort, and the brutality of their sufferings frequently appals us. While, moreover, there is a hint of strain in Ford's imagining of Calantha and her court, there is a touch of the facile in his presentation of Warbeck's resolution. This perhaps makes *Perkin Warbeck* a lesser play than *The Broken Heart*, just as Ford's work as a whole has not the broad humanity and unchecked vision that characterize the major plays of Webster.

It is probable that *Perkin Warbeck* was Ford's last tragedy. Certainly it was his most difficult dramatic task, to enrol among his personal aristocracy the impostor of low birth, followed by a rout of the greedy, the craven and the base. Though the play lacks the intensity and the hint of subtlety that can be found in *The Broken Heart*, it is in some ways the work that leads us most easily to an understanding of Ford's characteristic attitude. Its difference from Shakespeare's histories is due partly to the development of the 'private' theatre in the years following Shakespeare's retirement, and partly to the general change in the seventeenth-century dramatic temper. But the difference arises also from a special peculiarity of Ford. His was a simpler dramatic world than Shakespeare's, a simpler attitude to human conduct. Shakespeare found his examples of tragic greatness in a murderer like Macbeth, a great-hearted child like Othello, a man who loved, as Lear did, both ease and ceremony: he saw their imperfections along with their greatness: he saw, in a sense, the justice of each man's fate, and also its dreadful lack of mercy. In Shakespeare's tragedy, as we have seen, there is something of protest, something of regret. For Ford there is no protestation to be made: the march of events is of course irresistible, it is not to be regretted: the characters who win his praise are those who do not attempt resistance

but step grandly on to the scaffold. In *'Tis Pity* he could be
in two minds about Giovanni. He is not in two minds about
Bianca or Calantha or Warbeck or the other leading characters of these plays: they are all securely among his 'elect'.
If he ever doubts the possible existence of Calantha and her
court, he never allows their inherent goodness to be sharply
questioned. If indeed there is ever a latent uncertainty in his
view of this, it is something that the characters themselves
do not share. I have already spoken of his simplicity of
language. It is a telling simplicity that fits the characters'
assurance. Because they are confident of their values, as
Shakespeare's often were not, they can go to their deaths
with an aristocratic lack of dread. If the end comes quickly
or gently, it is their last but not their gravest trial. So Orgilus
shakes hands with time, so Warbeck dismisses the small fact
of his ending:

> Death? pish, 'tis but a sound; a name of air;
> A minute's storm, or not so much: to tumble
> From bed to bed, be massacred alive
> By some physicians, for a month or two,
> In hope of freedom from a fever's torments,
> Might stagger manhood; here the pain is past
> Ere sensibly 'tis felt. (V, iii.)

Ford's general indifference to event and process lead to an
effect of dislocation in his work. The writers of the first rank
can convince us on every level: in them, the movement of
the current of time, the interpolated moment of stillness,
and the totality within which the movement and the stillness are subsumed, have a like validity, and we can appreciate
King Lear, for example, on any level of consciousness. But
in Ford we must be dissatisfied with the surface-effect. We
must look beyond it—though to do so involves an effort.
If that can be managed, we may get from these three of his
tragedies a kind of experience similar to that offered to us
by Dostoievsky in *The Devils*, where events tumble hap-

hazardly from life's sleeve, but where uniform principles of being and virtue are strenuously affirmed. Ford's seems a small talent when we mention it along with Dostoievsky's, but these men are alike in the kind of barrier that separates them from the casual reader and in their power to suggest the insignificance of event.

Tragi-Comedy

CHAPTER FOUR

TRAGI-COMEDY

FROM the end of the first decade of the seventeenth century, one of the most popular dramatic forms was tragi-comedy. It was, however, not the 'mongrel tragi-comedy' that Sidney had despised in the drama of his time.[1] That had been a crude form of tragedy—at least in the sense that disaster came at the end for its protagonist—interspersed with farcical scenes that were for the most part 'comic relief'. Seventeenth-century tragi-comic writing was romantic rather than tragic: it showed the principal characters undergoing distress and danger during much of the play, but near the end a new turn was given to events and all worked out well. There might, in addition, be an infusion of the merely comic, but the characteristic feature of these plays is not a mingling of kinds but rather a displacement of the dramatic pattern. The displacement is commonly brought about by a revelation, both to the characters and to the audience, of a secret that has hitherto been well kept. Thus in Beaumont and Fletcher's *A King and No King* the king Arbaces falls in love with his sister Panthea: she reciprocates his love and, though both are horrified at the thought of incest, it appears that a disastrous relationship will be established between them: then in the last Act it is revealed that Arbaces and Panthea are not brother and sister, he is not the true king, she is most fortunately queen in her own right, and Arbaces can marry her. This kind of writing was firmly established through the work of Fletcher, and he had many successors in the later Jacobean and the Caroline years: Massinger and Shirley, Brome and Davenant, were

[1] *An Apology for Poetry (English Critical Essays (Sixteenth, Seventeenth, and Eighteenth Centuries)*, edited by E. D. Jones, 1922, p. 55).

only the most distinguished of those playwrights who taught their audiences to expect sudden revelations, ingenious avoidances of final disaster. There is no hint of irony in this, as we may find, for example, in the *Alcestis* of Euripides. The happy ending is delighted in as the establishment of a permanent good, with no awkward doubts concerning the reverberations of the characters' earlier behaviour. Clearly there was an opportunity for irony in such a dramatic action as that of *A King and No King*, but Fletcher and his successors were aiming not at all at their audience's discomfort. Fletcher himself gives us a hint every now and again that he was capable of seeing the irony of his dramatic situation —notably, I think, in his *Demetrius and Enanthe*, where Enanthe's ultimate reconciliation with Demetrius is not achieved without a wry glance at her latent willingness— but only rarely did he allow that to intrude on his final effect. An ironic conclusion belonged to an earlier generation, to Chapman in *The Widow's Tears*, to Jonson, and perhaps to the Shakespeare who did not always share his own characters' conviction that all was well ended.

But Shakespeare also wrote, at the end of his career, certain tragi-comedies that have some resemblance to Fletcher's. *Pericles*, *Cymbeline*, *The Winter's Tale*, *The Tempest* and *Henry VIII* are all plays in which there is much sadness in the current of the action: even death may overtake a Prince Mamillius or a Queen Katherine. But at the end all, or nearly all, is put right, with the reunion of families, the relief from long penance (in Posthumus and Leontes and Alonso) or from unmerited suffering (in Pericles and Hermione). The principal characters bear lives as charmed as Fletcher's kings and lovers, and they enter finally into a state of permanent blessedness. There are, however, important differences between Shakespeare's romances and those of Fletcher and his successors. Shakespeare, for one thing, is manifestly more serious in his approach to this kind of writing. Whatever our precise interpretation of his last plays may be, we can hardly deny that he considered himself engaged with important matters. His pictures of human suffering and human vice have an intensity and a genuineness that demand our respect, and his final scenes have often the atmosphere of a solemn rite. We are taken to the temple of Diana at Ephesus, to the remote place where Hermione's statue may become a living queen, to the celebration of Queen Elizabeth's birth and the Archbishop's prophecy of her greatness. This seriousness of manner is reinforced by Shakespeare's frequent use of divine intervention in these plays. It is the goddess Diana who directs Pericles to Ephesus, where his lost wife may be found; it is Jupiter who appears to Posthumus at the lowest point of his fortunes and in a riddling fashion promises that all will come well; it is Apollo's oracle that declares Hermione innocent; and in *The Tempest* the figures of the gods are brought in to do honour to Ferdinand and Miranda at their betrothal. Such a direct manifestation of the supernatural was hardly possible at the end of *Henry VIII*, but the Archbishop's prophetic utterance brings contact with a celestial order. In general, this supernatural element is not found in the tragi-comedies that derive from Fletcher. He and his successors were predominantly concerned with the making of a dramatic action that would surprise and excite. Shakespeare's last plays, on the other hand, suggest a world in which the natural and the supernatural planes can come into contact. It is not chance, or the playwright's skill, that brings about the ending: it is the work of Providence. Some of us may feel that the dramatist at times makes Providence behave rather strangely, and indeed that he has to make a palpable effort to credit the cosmology that he employs (just as we may feel a straining in Thomas Hardy to credit the cosmic machinery of his major novels), but that does not lessen the difference between the Shakespearian and Fletcherian tragi-comic modes.

Now the plays of Ford that we have yet to consider—*The Lover's Melancholy*; *The Queen, or The Excellency of her Sex*;

The Fancies Chaste and Noble; and *The Lady's Trial*—are also plays in which disastrous happenings seem very close to the characters but are finally averted. We have seen how well Ford knew his dramatic predecessors, and doubtless he realized the superficial resemblances between these plays and Fletcher's tragi-comedies, and between these plays and Shakespeare's. Yet we have seen him breaking free from the Jacobean tradition in tragedy and giving us, in *Love's Sacrifice* and *The Broken Heart* and *Perkin Warbeck*, a kind of tragic writing peculiar to himself. It is not surprising, therefore, that in the plays we are now to look at he explores an equally independent vein. His happy endings are not simply the result of chance or of the intervention of Providence. They are achieved, in *The Lover's Melancholy* and *The Queen*, through the contrivance of a man skilled in the nature of human distress and able to find a means to cure it. In *The Lady's Trial* it is primarily the firm resolution of the sufferer, Auria, that makes all come right. Only in *The Fancies* have we the kind of revelation that is characteristic of Fletcher. But *The Fancies* is a strange play, and we shall see that there was perhaps a special reason for Ford's taking refuge here in Fletcherian device.[1] In general we may say that this group of plays, more than any other in the seventeenth century, depends on a psychological examination of character, on a belief that human ingenuity can sometimes bring life back to a normal road. The dramatist makes free use of Burton's *Anatomy of Melancholy*, giving us indeed in *The Lover's Melancholy* a simple though moving illustration of Burton's theorizing. There is no suggestion in Ford, as of course there is no suggestion in Burton, that a specific course of treatment will always serve to put the mind right. At times, however, something can be done, and the dramatist takes pleasure in showing us what it is.

[1] Oliver, pp. 122-4, has clearly differentiated Ford's tragi-comedy from the Fletcherian type that was carried on by Massinger and many others in the Caroline years.

But he is no more consistent than we should expect a creative artist to be. Especially in *The Lover's Melancholy* he combines a dependence on Burton with a frequent asseveration that Providence watches and guides all. Indeed, as this play proceeds, references to Providence and its mercy grow more frequent. Near the beginning we have a typically Fordian comment on fate:

> 'Tis a fate
> That overrules our wisdoms; whilst we strive
> To live most free, we're caught in our own toils. (I, iii.)

And this comment is similarly neutral in its attitude:

> But in all actions nature yields to fate. (III, ii.)

But later fate has become a guide, a conscious power for good:

> in vain we strive to cross
> The destiny that guides us. (III, ii.)

And we find that a protective mercy enters the play's field of ideas:

> We are but fools
> To trifle in disputes, or vainly struggle
> With that eternal mercy which protects us. (IV, iii.)

In the last scene of the play we have this exchange between the physician Corax and Cleophila, the daughter of the distracted Meleander:

> *Cor.*   . . . O, lady, in the turmoils of our lives,
> Men are like politic states, or troubled seas,
> Toss'd up and down with several storms and tempests,
> Change and variety of wrecks and fortunes;
> Till, labouring to the havens of our homes,
> We struggle for the calm that crowns our ends.
>   *Cleo.* A happy end heaven bless us with!
>   *Cor.*   'Tis well said. (V, i.)

Then Meleander, recovered from his distraction, contrasts the littleness of man with the magnanimous Providence above him:

> O, what a thing is man,
> To bandy factions of distemper'd passions
> Against the sacred Providence above him! (V, i.)

And later:

> O, children, children, pay your prayers to heaven,
> For they have show'd much mercy. (V, i.)

Palador, the melancholy lover of the title, ends the play with grateful words to a fate which is clearly now indistinguishable from Providence:

> So they thrive
> Whom fate in spite of storms hath kept alive. (V, i.)

The main action of the play is simple. Palador, Prince of Cyprus, was in love with Eroclea, but his father pursued her lustfully and she fled from the island. Before the play begins, Palador has succeeded to the throne, but is stricken with melancholy through his loss of Eroclea: her father Meleander is also distracted with grief. The court physician attempts to cure Palador by devising a masque of melancholy, for which Ford marginally admits his indebtedness to Burton. This, however, avails nothing, and the cure of both Palador and Meleander is achieved when the lost Eroclea is brought once again to her lover and her father. At first, to fill out the action a little, she is brought to Cyprus in male disguise. A number of characters take part in the effecting of the cures: Menaphon, a friend of Palador, by discovering the disguised Eroclea on his travels; Corax, the court physician, and Rhetias, a cynical courtier, by their careful stage-management of Eroclea's appearance in her own attire. Ford implies that only a fortunate, or a Providential, turn of event (the discovery of Eroclea) could help Palador and Meleander in their misery, and that such chances may on occasion present themselves. In the dialogue, as we have seen, the share of Providence is stressed; in the action, however, our attention is drawn to the efforts of Corax and Rhetias, and their share in the ultimate success.

Though there is some laboured 'comic relief' and some rather tiresome complication of the serious action when the Princess Thamasta falls in love with the disguised Eroclea, the play as a whole has a compelling atmosphere. Without the frequent harshness of Shakespeare's last plays, it has something of their lyrical quality, of their delight in the contemplation of an achieved happiness.[1] In particular, the scene where Meleander awakes and finds Eroclea restored to him may remind us of Pericles' finding of Marina. Not that Ford echoes *Pericles* here: rather, he very clearly has in mind the scene in *Lear* where the king who has been mad returns to his senses in Cordelia's presence. Like Lear, Meleander has been sleeping and has had fresh garments put on him. Corax tells us:

> I drench'd his cup to purpose; he ne'er stirr'd
> At barber or at tailor. He will laugh
> At his own metamorphosis, and wonder.—
> We must be watchful. Does the couch stand ready? (V, i.)

As he awakes, Meleander's questions and his belief that he still dreams are put in words close to Lear's:

> Where am I? ha! What sounds are these? 'Tis day, sure.
> O, I have slept belike; 'tis but the foolery
> Of some beguiling dream. (V, i.)

And later he asks:

> Lend me a looking-glass.—How now! how came I
> So courtly, in fresh garments? (V, i.)

---

[1] '*The Lover's Melancholy* . . . could hardly have been written but for *Cymbeline*, *The Winter's Tale*, *Pericles*, and *The Tempest*' (T. S. Eliot, *Selected Essays*, p. 194).

Near the end he is, like Lear, conscious of his age and weakness, humble in his prayer not to be mocked:

> My brains are dull'd;
> I am entranc'd, and know not what you mean.
> Great, gracious sir, alas, why do you mock me?
> I am a weak old man, so poor and feeble,
> That my untoward joints can scarcely creep
> Unto the grave, where I must seek my rest. (V, i.)[1]

In Shakespeare's tragedy the reunion of the King and his daughter was not the end. It was an interval, a respite, some scrap of great treasure saved from the wreckage of human lives. Soon struggle and suffering and loss were to be again the dominant strains. Dr E. M. W. Tillyard has suggested that in Shakespeare's last plays we have a kind of dramatic writing that goes beyond tragedy, taking us out of the tragic negation into a world where atonement is made.[2] But that seems a partial account of what happens. Rather, Shakespeare in his last plays plans to bring his action to a finality at the point he had reached in *Lear* when the father and daughter met: stopping at that moment of reconciliation, he tries—with I think varying success—to offer it as a symbol of an ultimate reconciliation between man and the nature of things. Because his mind was so comprehensive, it

---

[1] It may well have been the echoes in these speeches and in the situation in Act V that led Charles Macklin (presumably) to allege that Jonson accused Ford of pillaging from Shakespeare. According to two letters sent by Macklin to the *General Advertiser* in April 1748, on the occasion of a revival of the play, Jonson stated that Ford merely revised *The Lover's Melancholy* after stealing the MS. from among Shakespeare's papers with the connivance of Hemminge and Condell. This story was strongly assailed by Malone in his Variorum Shakespeare, and its principal interest to-day is its curious underlining of the relationship between Ford's play and Shakespeare's final romances. (See Sargeaunt, pp. 25, 171; Davril, pp. 55-8; G. E. Bentley, *The Jacobean and Caroline Stage*, iii, 450-51.)

[2] *Shakespeare's Last Plays*, 1938, pp. 16-26.

was far more difficult for Shakespeare than for Ford to think in these terms of ultimate reconciliation: he could not help remembering the price that had been paid, he was not quite free from the tragic impulse of defiance, the reconciliation conveyed with it a suggestion of fatigue. But Ford could more easily narrow his view, particularly as—despite the references to Providence—there is little sense in *The Lover's Melancholy* that every Palador, every Meleander will have an Eroclea returned to them. All he is saying is that, with some individuals, some communities, there may be an opportunity to return to the road of health and there may be men ready and able to avail themselves of it. Then, and only then, a sick mind or a sick court may be made whole.

It was, moreover, of the very nature of Ford's tragic writing that defiance or resentment found no place in it. He was content, as we have seen, with the final gesture of a Calantha or a Warbeck, and this contentment could easily become a readiness to accept the chance blessings that life may offer or the more designed blessings of Providence. It was thus far easier for Ford to cultivate the attitude that informs *The Lover's Melancholy* than it was for Shakespeare to come to the writing of his last plays. Similarly it was possible for Ford to turn from *The Lover's Melancholy* to tragedy: it would be startling to imagine a Shakespearian tragedy that was later in date than *The Winter's Tale*.

The Queen, or The Excellency of her Sex is a less impressive play than *The Lover's Melancholy*, but it exhibits more clearly than they appear elsewhere certain aspects of Ford's world. It was published anonymously in 1653, and was not attributed to Ford until Professor Bang edited it in 1906.[1] The attribution is solely on grounds of style, but it has won general acceptance. At the beginning of the action Alphonso is under sentence of death for rebellion against the Queen. She pardons him on the scaffold and marries him. He

[1] *Materialen zur Kunde des älteren englischen Dramas*, xiii, Louvain 1906.

declares himself a hater of womankind, and insists on a delay
before marital relations are established. Then his follower
Muretto makes him jealous, suggesting that the Queen is
being unfaithful. Alphonso declares that she must die unless
a champion will fight on her behalf. When she is brought to
judgment, three champions appear—including Muretto,
who says that he has invented the story of infidelity in order
to make Alphonso jealous and thus appreciative of his wife's
beauty. Alphonso's woman-hating is thus cured, and he and
the Queen can be happy. There are some slackly written
comic scenes, involving characters of a lower order, and a
sub-plot concering Valasco, the Queen's general, and his
love for Salassa, a widow, whose delight in exercising power
over him leads her, with much improbability, to the scaffold.
Like Alphonso and the Queen, she too escapes at the last
moment. Certainly by the end of the play the audience
might be forgiven for thinking that in this dramatic world
everyone was safe from the fact of execution. As in *Love's
Sacrifice*, there is a close imitation here of Iago's prompting
of Othello to jealousy. It is rather more mechanically done
here, however, and Alphonso and Muretto have not the
necessary authority of character to prevent this kind of thing
from being comic:

Alph.   . . . Monstrous woman! Beast!
Were these the fruits of her dissembling tears!
Her puling, and her heart sighs. But, *Muretto*.
I will be swift *Muretto*, swift and terrible.
     Muret. I am such another Coxcomb; O my side too.
Yet faith, let me perswade ye; I hope your wife is vertuous.
     Alph. Vertuous? The Devil she is, 'tis most impossible.
What kiss and toy, wink, prate, yet be vertuous?
     Muret. Why not Sir? I think now a woman may lie four or
five nights together with a man, and yet be chast; though that
be very hard, yet so long as 'tis possible, such a thing may be.
     Alph. I have it, wee'll confer; let's stand aside. (III.)

There are also casual echoes of the comic scenes in *2 Henry IV* and *The Tempest*:

> *Pyn.* . . . Am I not *Pynto*, have *I* not hiren here? What art thou, a full moon, or a moon calf?
> *Buff.* No, no, 'tis a dry Stock-fish, that must be beaten tender. (III.)

It will be noted, too, that Ford is close to Fletcher in concealing Muretto's motive from the audience: we have a last-act surprise when Muretto appears, to put all right.

Nevertheless, as in *The Lover's Melancholy*, we have the successful treatment of a diseased mind. Alphonso's woman-hating is presented as a pathological condition, which leads him first into rebellion, because his country must not be governed by a woman, and then into an arrogant and venomous cruelty to the woman he has agreed to marry. At the same time the reader may wonder if, in this curious play, Ford's sympathies are not more deeply on Alphonso's side than at first appears. He has the resolution to die rather than to ask pardon, and he visibly diminishes in stature when he comes at last to feel jealousy and love. Moreover, the sub-plot reinforces this effect. Salassa makes Valasco vow not to engage in fight for two years or to explain why he has apparently deserted his profession of arms. This not merely brings him to indignity but prevents him from defending his Queen when she needs a champion. When, however, Salassa offers to release him from his vow, he says she has not the power to do so. As Salassa has pledged her life to produce Valasco as the Queen's champion, it is this course of events that leads her to the scaffold. Valasco, half-relenting, says he will break his vow but will no longer love Salassa. In the generally happy ending, he is persuaded to forgive her. In all this there is perhaps a hint of resentment against love's power over men, against the authority of women. Apart from *Perkin Warbeck* and the 'Jacobean' tragedy of *'Tis Pity She's a Whore*, Ford's dramatic world is dominated by women-characters, who are exalted for their beauty, their devotion, and their exquisite command of speech and gesture. The Queen in this play is one of their number, but she is a fainter image of their excellence. So it was perhaps possible here for certain feelings, normally kept below the level of direct avowal, to manifest themselves. Ford does not suggest to us in *Love's Sacrifice* that the beauty of Bianca is to be regretted, destroying the friendship of her husband and Fernando, and leading both men to death, or in *The Broken Heart* that Bassanes and Orgilus might have lived well enough if the frenzy of love had not come on them. But, if we look at these plays in a certain mood, it is such ideas that will come into our minds. And very possibly Ford's mind was not entirely proof against them. We shall see a hint of this too in *The Fancies Chaste and Noble*, where the impotent Octavio's continuing devotion to beauty is exhibited.

If this is so, *The Queen* may make us more conscious of the precariousness of Ford's hold on his ideal in *The Broken Heart* and *Love's Sacrifice*. We should be wrong to put a strong emphasis on this aspect of things, even in *The Queen*, where finally the cure of Alphonso is wrought and a woman's world is again exalted. The Queen's praise of marriage, linking it to Love and Fate and Divinity, recalls Penthea's permanent devotion to her lost Orgilus, Calantha's to her lost Ithocles:

> There is a holy league
> Confirm'd and ratify'd 'twixt Love and Fate.
> This sacred Matrimonial tye of hearts,
> Call'd marriage, has Divinity within 't. (III.)

Nevertheless, the play may hint at the force of the effort that has, successfully, gone to the making of Calantha's and Penthea's world.

In Chapter I, something was said of the main plot of *The*

Fancies Chaste and Noble. Livio, for the sake of advancement, is persuaded by Troylo-Savelli, nephew of Octavio, Marquess of Sienna, to have his sister Castamela enter the society of the Fancies, three young women who, according to Troylo-Savelli, are kept by the Marquess for his impotent delight. Livio repents of his acquiescence, but Castamela insists on keeping to the bargain. She is resolute in virtue, however, when the Marquess makes advances to her. When her disguised suitor Romanello gets admittance to the enclosed society, he is convinced of her depravity and abandons his suit. Then suddenly it is revealed that the three Fancies are the Marquess's nieces, whose virtuous education he has been supervising, that Castamela's virtue was being tried, and that Troylo-Savelli loves her. Livio is perfunctorily paired off with one of the Fancies. This highly Fletcherian last-act reversal is so surprising that Dr Ewing has been unable to believe it: he assumes that the Fancies were actually being kept by the Marquess for the purpose which Troylo-Savelli indicated to Livio, and which is indeed confirmed by the behaviour of the Marquess and his lewd servant Morosa.[1] But this simply will not cohere with the dénouement, dependent as it is on Troylo-Savelli's love for Castamela and Livio's marriage to one of the Fancies. What, I think, seems likely is that Ford has ended this play in a way remote from his original planning. When Troylo-Savelli first speaks of his uncle, we are meant to see another example of a diseased mental condition, analogous to Bassanes', Palador's, Meleander's, Alphonso's. Octavio is elderly and impotent. Both conditions were of interest to Ford: he had perhaps hinted at impotence in Bassanes,[2] and

[1] Ewing, pp. 48-50.
[2] Ewing, p. 58. But the point is by no means overtly made in the play: if it were, it would further complicate, perhaps, the relations of Orgilus and Penthea. Peter Ure, 'Marriage and the Domestic Drama in Heywood and Ford', *English Studies*, xxxii (1951), 200-16, has indeed drawn attention to passages in *The Broken Heart* which suggest that the marriage of Penthea and Bassanes was consummated.

on several occasions he studied the love-relations of the elderly—in Bassanes in *The Broken Heart*, in the Duke in *Love's Sacrifice*, and in Auria in *The Lady's Trial*. But in the nature of things there can be no cure for Octavio, unless he can be brought to reconcile himself to loss. That could have been suggested dramatically, but if the Fancies were as they were first described it would have been difficult for Ford to devise a satisfactory ending for them and Troylo-Savelli and Livio. So it looks as if Ford had decided, near the end of the play, to dispose of the whole situation by pretending that it never existed. Even if his change of mind were not so radical as this, he certainly imagined with peculiar force the situation of Octavio as described by his nephew. I have already pointed out the contrast between the way in which Octavio appears, both in his own behaviour and in Troylo-Savelli's account, and the grossness of his servants' jesting. His inclinations show a perversion of mind, but they remain aristocratic: his advances to Castamela when she has joined the society of the Fancies are restrained and courteous. This direction of our sympathy towards Octavio is reinforced by the general picture of social corruption which the play suggests. In the opening scene Troylo-Savelli draws the attention of Livio to the vile means by which men achieve advancement:

> *Troy.* . . . Look, prithee, through the Great Duke's court
>   in Florence,
> Number his favourites, and then examine
> By what steps some chief officers in state
> Have reach'd the height they stand in.
>   *Liv.*   By their merits.
>   *Troy.* Right, by their merits: well he merited
> Th' intendments o'er the galleys at Ligorne,—
> Made grand collector of the customs there,—
> Who led the prince unto his wife's chaste bed,
> And stood himself by in his night-gown, fearing

The jest might be discover'd: was't not handsome?
The lady knows not yet on't.
    Liv.   Most impossible.
    Troy. He merited well to wear a robe of chamlet
Who train'd his brother's daughter, scarce a girl,
Into the arms of Mont-Argentorato;
While the young lord of Telamon, her husband,
Was packeted to France to study courtship,
Under, forsooth, a colour of employment,—
Employment! yea, of honour.
    Liv.   You're well read
In mysteries of state.
    Troy.   Here in Sienna,
Bold Julio de Varana, lord of Camerine,
Held it no blemish to his blood and greatness
From a plain merchant with a thousand ducats
To buy his wife, nay, justify the purchase;
Procur'd it by a dispensation
From Rome, allow'd and warranted: 'twas thought
By his physicians that she was a creature
Agreed best with the cure of the disease
His present new infirmity then labour'd in.
Yet these are things in prospect of the world,
Advanc'd, employ'd, and eminent. (I, i.)

There had been denunciations of contemporary evil in *The Lover's Melancholy*, but there the suggestion was made that the ills were due to the Prince's melancholy and his dead father's criminality, things that could pass:

Our commonwealth is sick: 'tis more than time
That we should wake the head thereof, who sleeps
In the dull lethargy of lost security.
The commons murmur, and the nobles grieve;
The court is now turn'd antic, and grows wild,
Whiles all the neighbouring nations stand at gaze,

And watch fit opportunity to wreak
Their just-conceivèd fury on such injuries
As the late prince, our living master's father,
Committed against laws of truth or honour. (II, i.)

But in *The Fancies* the evil is not confined to Sienna, where
Octavio sickly rules, but is spread through Italy and, by
implication, the world. In that world Octavio's perversion
is not seen as a prime source of evil, but as a small and pitiful
condition. Moreover, one of the instances of misconduct
that Troylo-Savelli refers to is shown to us in detail in the
play's sub-plot. Flavia was the wife of Fabricio, a merchant,
but he was induced to sell her, legally it appears, to Julio,
lord of Camerino. She seems at first to be indifferent to the
transaction, and enters on her new life with levity. But it
becomes evident that she has endured grief and shame and a
deep sense of insecurity in her new marriage. Her first
husband, too, has come to a full realization of his guilt and,
leaving the world in which he has offended, will devote his
life to religion. Ford has not given to this plot the careful
treatment it deserved, and he has unsatisfactorily used a
Fletcherian technique in first presenting Flavia as wholly
light-minded, and suddenly explaining this by the suggestion that she considered an appearance of levity her only
safeguard in the courtly world she had entered. But he does
arouse our interest and our sympathy with Flavia, a woman
who has been placed in a position where her natural virtue
seems destroyed, but where, despite the corruption of her
world, she can behave with discretion and charity. Again,
as with Octavio, we are made to feel that the general circumstances are more evil than the characters brought prom-
inently before us. Flavia and her two husbands make their
peace with each other and with themselves, as best they may.
We could wish that Ford had had the persistence and perhaps
the courage to face Octavio's situation with an equal frank-
ness. It would, of course, have made the play difficult to

wind up. Moreover, an audience is not easily persuaded to give its sympathy to the impotent,[1] so it may have seemed safer to use the fashionable Fletcherian technique and thus attempt to banish all consideration of Octavio's alleged practice. Critics of Ford usually turn from this play after the briefest comment on it, with the expression of a wish that it had not been written. It is manifestly unsatisfactory as a whole, but in the situations of Flavia and Octavio it touches on aspects of life that Ford could evidently and powerfully imagine. We should wish, not that it had not been written, but that its subjects had been faced with more resolution.[2]

The Lady's Trial would be a suitable title for several of Ford's independent plays. Yet in the main action of what was probably his last play the central figure, the character who resolutely brings affairs to a good ending, is a man.[3] Auria, it appears, is somewhat elderly and has recently married a young wife, Spinella. He is poor and, leaving her, goes to find fame and fortune in the wars. In his absence the lord Adurni attempts to seduce her: Auria's friend Aurelio finds Adurni and Spinella together behind locked doors, and tells Auria of this on his triumphant return. Spinella for a time hides herself, being outraged by Aurelio's assumption of her guilt. But her husband, though troubled, insists on hearing the evidence dispassionately and is at length persuaded of her innocence. It is a simple story, presented in a

[1] A dramatist of this century who managed the task was Prince Antoine Bibesco, who in *The Heir* (1932) presented a main character with some resemblance to Ford's Octavio.

[2] If G. E. Bentley (*The Jacobean and Caroline Stage*, iii, 444) is right in his suggestion that *The Fancies* was first written in 1631 and that a revision was made in 1635-6, it is possible that the Fletcherian transformation was brought into the play at the later date.

[3] Davril, p. 226, has noted that Malfato, a minor character who is vainly in love with Spinella, cures himself by resolutely facing his situation. In this he recalls Bassanes in *The Broken Heart*, but it is more important that he provides in the subordinate action of *The Lady's Trial* an echo of Auria's ministry to his own mind.

series of debates and investigations. Inevitably its dramatic interest is not intense, but the sobriety of the play, brought to a focal point in the conduct of Auria, commands our respect. Certainly it is far in spirit from the popular tragi-comedies contemporary with it. There are sub-plots involving the wantonness and repentance of Levidolche, a cast mistress of Adurni, and the affectations of Amoretta, whose comic appeal depends mainly on her lisping. Ford's consciousness of gentility comes out rather embarrassingly when, after Levidolche's repentance, she is condescendingly given alms by Adurni, Spinella and Castanna, Spinella's sister. The playwright was indeed little concerned with his subordinate actions here, the conduct of the Levidolche plot defying probability even more grossly than is Ford's custom with sub-plots. He was, as ever, convinced of the higher importance of his noble characters. At one moment in the play the embittered Malfato has levelling thoughts:

> *Mal.* . . . I read no difference between this huge,
> This monstrous big word 'lord' and 'gentleman',
> More than the title sounds; for aught I learn,
> The latter is as noble as the first,
> I'm sure more ancient.
> *Aurel.* Let me tell you, then,
> You are too bitter, talk you know not what.
> Make all men equals, and confound all course
> Of order and of nature! this is madness.
> *Mal.* 'Tis so; and I have reason to be mad,— (I, iii.)

but his levelling goes no lower than the rank of 'gentleman'. Moreover, he quickly acknowledges his fault and the high status of nobility:

> In colder blood,
> I do confess nobility requires
> Duty and love; it is a badge of virtue,
> By action first acquir'd, and next in rank
> Unto anointed royalty. (I, iii.)

In the play's last scene, before Auria has fully convinced himself of his wife's fidelity, he addresses her in terms that have been recognized as owing something to Othello's comment on his and Desdemona's disparity in age and the consequent likelihood of her infidelity[1]:

> behold these hairs,
> Great masters of a spirit, yet they are not
> By winter of old age quite hid in snow;
> Some messengers of time, I must acknowledge,
> Amongst them took up lodging; when we first
> Exchang'd our faiths in wedlock, I was proud
> I did prevail with one whose youth and beauty
> Deserv'd a choice more suitable in both.
> Advancement to a fortune could not court
> Ambition either on my side or hers;
> Love drove the bargain, and the truth of love
> Confirm'd it, I conceiv'd. But disproportion
> In years amongst the married is a reason
> For change of pleasures: whereto I reply,
> Our union was not forc'd, 'twas by consent;
> So then the breach in such a case appears
> Unpardonable. (V, ii.)

So we find that Ford, after echoing *Othello* in *Love's Sacrifice* and *The Queen*, comes back to Shakespeare's play once more. But it is no longer a mere echo, no far-off reverberation of Othello's jealousy and torment. Auria is, as near as a loving and doubtful husband may be, dispassionate. There is a great quietness in him, a readiness to take into account every argument for or against Spinella. And his calmness is re-warded when at length it enables him to see her fidelity, the justification of his choice. The play is not exciting as *'Tis Pity* or *The Broken Heart* is exciting. It is in its sub-plots a poor thing, and in its main plot lacking in suspense and in

[1] Gifford-Dyce, iii, 90, n. 7.

richness of characterization. But there is much worth in the ideal of conduct presented in the figures of Auria and Spinella. She is sure of her own love, her own virtue, and does not seek pity; he is neither sanguine nor credulous. If we want to see an image of the way in which people may be driven to conduct themselves, finding each his own private hell, we shall look to the tragedy *Othello*. Ford's play is much smaller than that, in many ways too a play hardly competent in its management, but it does suggest a form of human aspiration, a civilized approach to the relations of human beings to one another. Perhaps because it came at the end of Ford's career, there is a sense of fatigue in it. We may, however, suspect that Auria's situation was one very close to Ford's heart. Auria was not young, and doubtful of the effect of his age on Spinella's love, yet his scrutiny of her was careful and did not lead him to throw a pearl away. The echo of *Othello* may have been intended for the audience to recognize. It is to Auria's credit as a representative of mankind that he did not behave like the Moor.

Apart from the evidence of a few contemporary references and the commendatory verses published with the plays, we know little of how Ford's work was regarded in his lifetime. His independent plays were acted at the Phoenix and the Blackfriars theatres: some at least of them must have established themselves in the repertory, for *'Tis Pity She's a Whore* and *The Lady's Trial* were revived after the Restoration. There have been few performances since.[1] Beyond question the plays are worth more assiduous attention than our theatres have given them, but we can never expect Ford to win great popularity. Despite Professor Sensabaugh's plea for him as a 'modern', the manner of his writing and the cast of his thought are indissolubly linked to the condition of his time. The age of Charles I was a strange one in many ways: the theatre for which Ford wrote belonged to a small section of the community, a section that cultivated its

[1] For the stage-history of the plays, see Appendix B.

own graces and could not credit the political changes that were beginning to manifest themselves. The drama looked often for its settings in remote places and times, yet it was an insular drama dependent on a court fashion that was, in the European context, provincial. The writers and their audience were conscious of their sophistication, yet they leaned greatly on earlier dramatic models, above all on Shakespeare and Fletcher and Jonson. Apart from Ford, the best dramatists of the time were the best imitators—Shirley capturing a little of the Jacobean manner, though not much of its spirit, in *The Cardinal*, and developing the modish comedy of Fletcher in *The Witty Fair One* and a long series of later plays; Brome following his master Jonson in the vigorous display of human eccentricity, human entanglements; Massinger at his best presenting a Christianized version of Chapman's stoicism; and all of them, along with Davenant and others, writing tragi-comedy according to the Fletcherian formula. Ford, too, we have seen, was influenced by the Jacobeans. He began in association with Dekker, and was clearly under the elder writer's influence in *The Witch of Edmonton* and *The Sun's Darling*. In *'Tis Pity She's a Whore* he attempts, and with success, to bring the spirit of Jacobean tragedy into the Caroline theatre, and in all his major plays it is evident that his memories of Shakespeare—particularly of *Othello*, *Lear* and *Romeo and Juliet*—are strong. Yet, though *'Tis Pity* is perhaps his most striking achievement, the play best fitted for later revival because least dependent on peculiar Caroline conditions, it is in the other tragedies and in the plays of which I have spoken in this last chapter that we shall find the essence of his genius most apparent. He had a profound understanding of suffering, and an ability to present it in dramatic poetry; he had a deep interest in abnormal conditions of the mind, using Burton as a source of information but not merely as a text-book that he was illustrating; he had a high ideal of human conduct, a reverence for love and fidelity and the relation of man and woman in true marriage.[1] Certainly his view of society was intensely class-conscious, and his ideal human being, though far removed from any conceivable norm, was in essence a courtier who would win King Charles's praise. That may be far from what is acceptable to-day: an easy and indiscriminate good-fellowship is not the way of his world. But we shall do ourselves an injustice if we deprive ourselves of what he has to offer. From *The Broken Heart* in particular we have a sense that a whole pattern of human experience is displayed for our awe and our affection. We know that we are not Calantha, Princess of Sparta, or Ithocles, her victorious general and her lover, but—if we can make the necessary effort of the historical imagination—we can recognize that they are what we can legitimately dream of being. The effect is like that of great sculpture—an effect of nobility, of the arrest of time, and of a universal human significance. Ford's dramatic range was narrow, and he came to grief when he ventured outside it. In contrivance he was often careless and perfunctory. His imaginative structures are fragile, and would not always be safe from mockery. But at his best—and in nearly every one of his plays he momentarily reaches his best—he dignifies not only human passion but the human condition.

Above all, he was a poet, not only in his conceptions but in his words. The playhouse of Charles I's time did not encourage an older-fashioned rhetoric, or the use of the compressed or violent image. The tone of the speaking had to be quieter, more attuned to the narrower, more courtly

[1] It is strange to read in a current publication: 'Ford's indifference to public values, however, marks a further degree in the social conversion of tragedy. Above all, it marks the dissolution of tragedy as an art, since the poet has no objective standard of judgment remaining to check his liquefying emotions' (L. G. Salingar, 'The Decline of Tragedy' in *The Age of Shakespeare*, edited by Boris Ford, 1955, p. 438). The values and the standard of judgment that led to an admiration for Warbeck and Calantha were indeed 'public' and 'objective'—certainly in relation to Ford's own social group, but also in a more enduring sense.

audience. But Ford knew how to secure the moving power of imagery, especially the imagery drawn from common life, while assiduously cultivating a simple fluency and melody of language. He resisted the tendency of his time to break down the structure of blank verse: his lines are more regular, less often run-on or with feminine endings, than those of most Caroline playwrights.[1] He knew that the exalted presentation of humanity needed a language that was manifestly different, though not wholly divorced, from that of the nearest actuality. He was writing in a time when poetic drama was in decay, and he showed what could be done by a playwright whose purpose needed poetry but would have been ruined by an ostentatious display of the merely 'poetic'. As a model of style, if for no other reason, he has an enduring value.

[1] Sargeaunt, p. 162; Davril, pp. 460-71.

LIST OF FORD'S WRITINGS

(i)

Non-Dramatic Writings

The following list includes a number of writings which have, with greater or less show of probability, been attributed to Ford. The items are arranged in chronological order of publication.

Fames Memoriall, or The Earle of Deuonshire Deceased: With his honourable life, peacefull end, and solemne Funerall (1606). A MS. of the poem, differing in some respects from the printed version, is in the Malone Collection in the Bodleian Library.[1]

Honor Trivmphant. Or The Peeres Challenge, by Armes defensible, at Tilt, Turney, and Barriers. In Honor of all faire Ladies, and in defence of these foure positions following. 1. Knights in Ladies seruice haue no free will. 2. Beauty is the mainteiner of valour. 3. Faire Lady was neuer false. 4. Perfect Louers are onely wise. Mainteined by Arguments. Also The King of Denmarkes welcome into England (1606).

Commendatory verses in Barnabe Barnes's *Foure Bookes of Offices* (1606).

A poem to the memory of the Earl of Devonshire, in John Cooper's *Funeral Teares for the death of the Earle of Deuonshire* (1606). The attribution to Ford was made by the antiquary Joseph Hunter in his *Chorus Vatum*.[2]

---

[1] Bertram Lloyd, 'An Inedited MS. of Ford's *Fames Memoriall*', *Review of English Studies*, i (January 1925), 93–5.

[2] Davril, p. 68.

Christes Bloodie Sweat, or the Sonne of God in his Agonie, By I. F. (1613). On the authorship of this poem, see above, p. 22. There was a second edition in 1616.

The Golden Meane. Lately written, as occasion serued, to a great Lord. Discoursing The Noblenesse of perfect Vertue in extreames (1613). On the authorship of this pamphlet, see above, pp. 24-5. There was a second edition, containing additional passages, in 1614, and a third in 1638.

The Characters of 'The Wise Man' and 'The Noble Spirit' (Nos. 12 and 13) which appeared among the Characters added to the second posthumous edition of Overbury's *The Wife* (1614). Ford's authorship has been suggested by Professor Davril, on the grounds of his known connection with Overbury, of the close association of nobility and wisdom in these two Characters and in Ford's known prose writings, and of certain parallels in phrasing and idea.[1] This attribution is very possibly correct, but the evidence does not compel belief.

'A booke called, *Sir Thomas Overburyes Ghost contayneinge the history of his life and vntimely death* by John Fford gent.' (Stationers' Register, 25 November 1615). This is not extant.

Commendatory verses in *Sir Thomas Ouerburie His Wife* (1616).

A Line of Life. Pointing at the Immortalitie of a Vertuous Name (1620). A MS. of this pamphlet, probably in the same hand as that of *Fames Memoriall*,[2] is in the British Museum (MS. Lansd. 350).

Commendatory verses in John Webster's *The Tragedy of the Dutchesse of Malfy* (1623).

Commendatory verses in Henry Cockram's *The English Dictionarie* (1623).

---

[1] *Ibid.*, pp. 91-7.
[2] Oliver, pp. 18-19. Mr Oliver believes that both these MSS. are presentation copies, the work of a professional copyist.

Commendatory verses in James Shirley's *The Wedding* (1629).

Commendatory verses in Philip Massinger's *The Roman Actor* (1629).

Commendatory verses in Richard Brome's *The Northern Lasse* (1632). It has been pointed out by Professor Davril that these verses were possibly the work of John Ford of Gray's Inn, cousin of the dramatist.[1]

Commendatory verses in Philip Massinger's *The Great Duke of Florence* (1636).

'On the best of English Poets, Ben: Ionson, Deceased', in *Ionsonus Virbius: or, The Memorie of Ben: Johnson Revived by the Friends of the Muses* (1638).

Commendatory verses in Edmund Elys's *Dia Poemata: Poetick Feet standing upon Holy Ground* (1655). These verses are signed 'Jo: Ford', and Elys's father was rector of East Alington, near Ilsington in Devonshire, where Ford may have lived during his last years. The verses, however, are so bad as to induce a doubt of his authorship. Miss Sargeaunt suggests he was deliberately imitating Elys's own manner,[2] but Professor Davril has understandably found this difficult to credit.[3]

A Contract of Love and Truth', a verse-anagram on the marriage of Mary Noel, daughter of Viscount Campden, and Sir Erasmus de la Fountaine, included in MS. Eg. 2725. The poem is signed 'J. Foord', and the MS. is a poetical miscellany of the second quarter of the seventeenth century. Mr Bertram Lloyd, in arguing for Ford's authorship, suggests the poem was written by the lawyer-dramatist for one of his clients.[4]

---

[1] Davril, p. 54, n. 34, referring to C. E. Andrews, *Richard Brome, A Study of His Life and Work*, New York 1913, pp. 20-1.

[2] Sargeaunt, p. 30.

[3] Davril, p. 62, n. 60.

[4] 'An Unprinted Poem by John Ford (?)', *Review of English Studies*, i (April 1925), 217-19. Sargeaunt, p. 29, regards Ford's authorship as highly probable.

(ii)

Dramatic Writings

The following lists are arranged, as far as knowledge permits, in chronological order of composition. For list (c), however, external evidence of dating is meagre.

(a) Lost Plays (including some of doubtful authorship)

An ill begining has a good end, & a bad begining may have a good end, a comedy entered by Humphrey Moseley in the Stationers' Register on 29 June 1660 and there attributed to Ford. Warburton's list of lost plays includes *A good beginning may have A good end*, which he likewise attributes to Ford. *A badd beginininge* [*sic*] *makes a good endinge* was acted by the King's men at court in 1612-13.[1] Professor T. M. Parrott has pointed out that Moseley was unreliable in his ascriptions, and that Sir Walter Greg has demonstrated Warburton's dependence on Moseley. The list of King's men's plays performed at court in 1612-13 consists, apart from *A badd beginininge*, of plays by Shakespeare, Jonson and Fletcher: Professor Parrott thinks it unlikely that with these they would include a play by the entirely unknown Ford. It is far more likely that Ford's dramatic career began with his collaboration with Dekker.[2]

The Fairy Knight, licensed by Herbert on 11 June 1624, probably for the Prince's company, with an attribution to Ford and Dekker.[3] The Folger Shakespeare Library has a MS. of *The Ffary Knight or Oberon the Second*, a play in prose. Professor Fredson Bowers has made a substantial

---

[1] E. K. Chambers, *The Elizabethan Stage*, iii, 315-16.

[2] 'A Note on John Ford', *Modern Language Notes*, lviii (April 1943), 247-53.

[3] J. Q. Adams, *The Dramatic Records of Sir Henry Herbert*, 1927, p. 29.

case for regarding this as the work of Thomas Randolph, probably written for performance at Westminster School when he was still a pupil there: the original composition is probably to be dated 1623 or 1624, but it was revised by another hand subsequent to 1637.[1] It may, Professor Bowers suggests, have owed something to the Ford and Dekker play: if so, Randolph's work must have deliberately taken over the title of the theatre-play, and the date 1624 can be assigned to it.

A Late Murther of the Sonn upon the Mother, licensed by Herbert in September 1624, with an attribution to Ford and Webster.[2] The alternative title of this play, referring to the comic plot, was *Keep the Widow Waking*. The comic plot was the work of Dekker and Rowley, and the performance at the Red Bull, perhaps by Prince Charles's men,[3] in 1624 led to Star Chamber proceedings.[4]

The Bristowe Merchant, licensed by Herbert on 22 October 1624, for the Palsgrave's company, with an attribution to Ford and Dekker.[5] Chambers suggested that this is identical with *The London Merchant*, which is assigned to Ford in Moseley's and Warburton's lists.[6]

Beauty in a Trance, entered in the Stationers' Register by Moseley on 9 September 1653, and there attributed to Ford. Warburton repeats the attribution. The play was acted at court by the King's men on 28 November 1630,[7]

---

[1] *The Fary Knight, or Oberon the Second*, edited by Fredson Bowers (*University of Virginia Studies*, No. 2), Chapel Hill, North Carolina, 1942. Cf. Fredson T. Bowers, 'Ben Jonson, Thomas Randolph, and *The Drinking Academy*', *Notes and Queries*, clxxiii (4 September 1937), 166-8.

[2] J. Q. Adams, *op. cit.*, p. 29.

[3] G. E. Bentley, *The Jacobean and Caroline Stage*, i, 209.

[4] C. J. Sisson, *Lost Plays of Shakespeare's Age*, 1936, pp. 80-124.

[5] J. Q. Adams, *op. cit.*, p. 30.

[6] *The Elizabethan Stage*, iii, 316.

[7] G. E. Bentley, *op. cit.*, i, 28.

and was included in the list of King's men's plays that on 7 August 1641 the Lord Chamberlain instructed the Stationers were not to be printed without the consent of the players.[1]

The Royall Combate, entered in the Stationers' Register by Moseley on 29 June 1660, and there attributed to Ford. Warburton repeats the attribution.

The Great Favourite, or The Duke of Lerma was acted and published as the work of Sir Robert Howard in 1668.[2] It has been suggested by Professor Alfred Harbage that this is an example of a Restoration re-writing of an early seventeenth-century play. Dryden in his *Defence of an Essay* seems to hint that Howard was not the real author, and Howard himself says that 'a gentleman brought a play to the King's Company, called *The Duke of Lerma*', which Howard read at the players' request and then adapted. In his account of the matter Howard refers to the original version as an 'old play', which must indicate a date of composition before 1642. The historical events in the play extend to the year 1629.[3] Professor Harbage finds that the extant version 'bears the stamp of Ford in its plot materials, its characters, and its style'. There is some resemblance in plot to *The Fancies*; chastity, as so often in Ford, is exposed to danger; Maria in *The Great Favourite* disappears from sight in the same fashion as Spinella in *The Lady's Trial*; Philip falls into a lethargy as a result of his love, like Palador in *The Lover's Melancholy*; the characters alternate between vehemence and tenderness, between weeping and intellectual calm; there are some verbal parallels with Ford's known plays. Professor Harbage has thus made a substantial case for the view that Howard's

---

[1] *Ibid.*, i, 65.
[2] See above, pp. 81-4.
[3] Oliver, p. 133, questions this and suggests 1624. For Mr Oliver's doubt of Ford's authorship, see above, p. 84, n. 1.

version preserves a good deal of a lost play by Ford, possibly that noted above as *Beauty in a Trance*.[1]

(b) *Extant Plays written in Collaboration*

The Witch of Edmonton: A known true Story. Composed into A Tragi-Comedy By divers well-esteemed Poets; William Rowley, Thomas Dekker, John Ford, &c. (1658), acted by the Prince's men at the Phoenix in 1621, and at court on December 29 in that year.[2] It was probably revived in 1635 or 1636 by the Queen's men.[3]

The Spanish Gipsie (1661), acted by the Lady Elizabeth's company at the Phoenix in 1623 and at court on 5 November 1623.[4] The title-page also refers to performance at Salisbury Court, where the company was presumably the Queen's. In 1639 the play was the property of Beeston's boys.[5] Though H. D. Sykes claimed the whole play for Ford, it seems more likely that it was written in collaboration.[6] It is assigned to Middleton and Rowley on the title-page.

The Welsh Embassador, probably written in 1623. The play is preserved in a MS. in the Cardiff Public Library and was published in the *Malone Society Reprints* in 1920. It was attributed to Dekker in a list of his plays compiled about 1678 by Alexander Hill. Mr Bertram Lloyd has supported this by noting parallels of style, and has found Ford's hand in two scenes.[7] The joint authorship is accepted by Mr

[1] Alfred Harbage, 'Elizabethan-Restoration Palimpsest', *Modern Language Review*, xxxv (July 1940), 287-319. G. F. Sensabaugh, 'Another Play by John Ford', *Modern Language Quarterly*, iii (December 1942), 595-601, has supported Harbage's case by referring to the influence on *The Great Favourite* of Burton and the Platonic-love cult, but Davril, p. 522, n. 8, has pointed out the fragility of this argument.

[2] G. E. Bentley, *op. cit.*, i, 205, 213.

[3] *Ibid.*, i, 251; iii, 272.   [4] *Ibid.*, i, 185, 186, 194.

[5] *Ibid.*, i, 255, 331, 340.   [6] See above, p. 32.

[7] 'The Authorship of *The Welsh Embassador*', *Review of English Studies*, xxi (July 1945), 192-201.

H. J. Oliver, who has suggested that the two dramatists may have been revising an earlier Dekker play.[1]

The Sun's Darling: A Moral Masque (1656), licensed by Herbert on 3 March 1624.[2] The original company was the Lady Elizabeth's men, but the play was the property of Beeston's boys in 1639.[3] The title-page assigns it to Ford and Dekker and refers to performance at court and at the Phoenix. Discounting the view that the play was a revision of Dekker's *Phaeton*,[4] Mr Oliver draws attention to the evidence that our text is a revision made in 1638 or 1639.[5] A second issue of the Quarto appeared in 1657.

The Faire Maide of the Inne, printed in the Beaumont and Fletcher Folio (1647), having been licensed by Herbert on 22 January 1626 for performance by the King's men at the Blackfriars.[6] Mr F. L. Lucas has argued for Ford's authorship of IV, i,[7] as suggested by H. D. Sykes.[8] The case, which is a reasonably strong one, is supported by Miss Sargeaunt.[9]

The Chances, The Sea-voyage, The Faithful Friends, Love's Pilgrimage and *The Laws of Candy* are other 'Beaumont and Fletcher' plays in which Ford's hand has at times been guessed at.[10] A reasonable case has been made out only for *The Laws of Candy*, published in the 1647 Folio: its probable date of composition is 1619-22.[11]

---

[1] Oliver, pp. 34-7.

[2] J. Q. Adams, *op. cit.*, p. 27.

[3] G. E. Bentley, *op. cit.*, i, 195, 331.

[4] See above, p. 36, n. 5.

[5] Oliver, pp. 39-40. Cf. G. E. Bentley, *op. cit.*, iii, 461.

[6] J. Q. Adams, *op. cit.*, p. 31.

[7] *The Complete Works of John Webster*, edited by F. L. Lucas, 1927, iv, 148-52. Cf. E. H. C. Oliphant, *The Plays of Beaumont and Fletcher*, 1927, pp. 463-72.

[8] *Sidelights on Elizabethan Drama*, 1924, p. 150.

[9] Sargeaunt, pp. 64-6.

[10] Cf. E. H. C. Oliphant, *op. cit.*, pp. 137, 249, 355, 432-3, 463-72.

[11] *Ibid.*, p. 476. Davril, p. 65, finds no trace of Ford in the play.

(c) *Extant Plays written Independently*

'Tis Pitty Shee's a Whore (1633): the title-page indicates performance by the Queen's men at the Phoenix. The play was the property of Beeston's boys in 1639.[1] For evidence that it was Ford's first independent play, see above, p. 49, n. 1.

The Lovers Melancholy (1629): the title-page indicates performance by the King's men at the Blackfriars and the Globe. The play was licensed by Herbert on 24 November 1628.[2]

Loues Sacrifice (1633): the title-page indicates performance by the Queen's men at the Phoenix. The play was the property of Beeston's boys in 1639.[3]

The Broken Heart (1633): the title-page indicates performance by the King's men at the Blackfriars.

The Chronicle Historie of Perkin Warbeck. A Strange Truth (1634): the title-page indicates performance by the Queen's men at the Phoenix.

The Queen, or The Excellency of Her Sex. An Excellent old Play. Found out by a Person of Honour, and given to the Publisher, Alexander Goughe (1653). For evidence of Ford's authorship, see above, p. 109.

The Fancies Chast and Noble (1638): the title-page indicates performance by the Queen's men at the Phoenix: this must have been before 12 May 1636, when the Queen's men left that theatre.[4] Professor Bentley has suggested, as a possibility, that the play was first acted in 1631 and revised in 1635-6.[5]

The Ladies Triall (1639): the title-page indicates performance by Beeston's boys at the Phoenix. The play was licensed by Herbert on 3 May 1638.[6]

[1] G. E. Bentley, *op. cit.*, i, 252, 331. [2] J. Q. Adams, *op. cit.*, p. 32.
[3] G. E. Bentley, *op. cit.*, i, 252, 331.
[4] Sargeaunt, p. 25. Cf. G. E. Bentley, *op. cit.*, i, 236-7.
[5] See above, p. 117, n. 2. [6] J. Q. Adams, *op. cit.*, p. 38.

FORD ON THE STAGE

In Appendix A we have noted evidence for the revival of some of Ford's plays before the closing of the theatres (*The Witch of Edmonton, The Sun's Darling*, and possibly *The Fancies Chaste and Noble*), and have seen that some remained sufficiently valuable dramatic property for their ownership to be stated some years after their first performance (*Beauty in a Trance, The Spanish Gipsy, The Sun's Darling, 'Tis Pity She's a Whore, Love's Sacrifice*). Apart, however, from the second issue of *The Sun's Darling* in 1657, not one of his plays was reprinted in the seventeenth century. Nor do we find them much referred to. Writing on *'Tis Pity She's a Whore*, Professor Bentley has remarked: 'there is no evidence that this or any other of his tragedies attracted much attention in the seventeenth century',[1] and indeed this observation need not have been limited to the tragedies. In the following short account are brought together all available references to stage-performances of Ford's plays from 1660 onwards, and until very recent years the story is one of almost uniform neglect. Adaptations and imitations of Ford plays will also be noticed.

(i) *1660–1700*

The only Ford play which we know to have been performed more than once in the Restoration years is *'Tis Pity*. A copy of the 1633 Quarto with MS. prompt notes was offered for sale in 1940: as the description of these notes in the bookseller's catalogue stated that 'scenic changes' were

[1] *The Jacobean and Caroline Stage*, iii, 462.

marked, it is likely that the performance in view was a Restoration one.[1] Certainly Pepys saw the play at Salisbury Court on 9 September 1661, after some heavy drinking: he found it 'a simple play and ill acted', but was pleased with the lady who sat beside him.[2] Soon afterwards we have record of a provincial performance: Edward Browne in his 'Memorandum Book, 1662' records seeing the play at the King's Arms, Norwich, in 1662 or the following year.[3]

The Lady's Trial is the one other Ford play which was certainly acted in the Restoration theatre. Pepys saw it at the Duke of York's playhouse on 3 March 1669, weary with late dancing on the night before. He found it 'but a sorry play'.[4]

The Broken Heart and The Lover's Melancholy were in the list of plays allotted to Davenant on 20 August 1668,[5] but there is no evidence that he put either on the stage.

It is possible, however, that a performance of Perkin Warbeck was at least planned. A MS. copy of the play is in the Bodleian Library, with initials (apparently indicating actors) before the names of the dramatis personae. It appears to be based on the 1634 Quarto, with numerous alterations. The hand is late seventeenth century according to Professor Davril, late seventeenth or early eighteenth according to Professor Bentley. Professor Davril has made the suggestion that the MS. version was prepared 'vers l'époque de l'affaire Monmouth'; Professor Bentley wonders if it has a connection with the performance in 1745.[6]

That in this period Ford could be remembered by a fellow-dramatist, though a mediocre one, is indicated by Sir Aston Cockain's The Tragedy of Ovid, published in 1662 as 'Intended to be Acted shortly'. Montague Summers

---

[1] The Jacobean and Caroline Stage, iii, 464.
[2] Sargeaunt, p. 170.
[3] The Jacobean and Caroline Stage, iii, 462.
[4] Sargeaunt, p. 170.
[5] Allardyce Nicoll, A History of English Drama 1660–1900, i (1952), 353.
[6] Davril, p. 184, n. 87; The Jacobean and Caroline Stage, iii, 456.

pointed out a few of the borrowings in this play from *The Broken Heart*,[1] and indeed Cockain's dependence on Ford is so great that he must have assumed there was little prospect of *The Broken Heart* itself being acted at this time. *The Tragedy of Ovid* has its scene in Pontus during Ovid's exile: he appears frequently but takes little part in the action, which is centred on the marriage of Bassanes and Clorina. She is loved by Pyrontus, and Bassanes becomes needlessly jealous and locks her in her chamber. When he believes her guilty, he kills Pyrontus, fastens Clorina in a chair and forces Pyrontus's heart into her hands. She dies of grief. The name of Bassanes, the locking of the door, the chair and the death of Clorina are clearly from *The Broken Heart*, the extracted heart of Pyrontus is as clearly from *'Tis Pity*. A minor character is called Spinella, thus echoing *The Lady's Trial*. Bassanes is accused of starving Clorina, while Penthea in *The Broken Heart* had refused to eat. There are several references to breaking hearts, and Ford's common image of an infected or ulcerous soul that must be cleansed appears twice:

> Thou hast a soul
> So ulcerous, Clorina, that the prayers
> And vows of all the world can never cleanse it. (IV, ii.)

> Her reputation's gone, for ever lost:
> A sea of tears cannot wash off her guilt.
> 'Tis so infectious, I am tainted with it. (IV, ii.)

The comment on Clorina's death ('She hath took leave of life!') is close to that on Orgilus's death in *The Broken Heart* ('He has shook hands with time'). There is no evidence that Cockain's play reached the stage, but at least we can be sure that Ford retained a reader in this dramatist, who wished in his own fashion to work Ford's vein in the theatre of his time.

[1] *The Playhouse of Pepys*, 1935, p. 246.

(ii) *1700-1890*

The only Ford performances that have been traced from the beginning of the eighteenth century to nearly the end of the nineteenth are that of *Perkin Warbeck* at Goodman's Fields on 19 December 1745[1] and that of *The Lover's Melancholy* at Drury Lane on 28 April 1748.[2] The 1745 rebellion, according to an Oldys note in Langbaine, occasioned the writing of two new plays on the Warbeck story, but Ford's was revived before either of them reached the stage.[3] The performance of *The Lover's Melancholy*, which was for Mrs Macklin's benefit, was the occasion of Macklin's letters to the *General Advertiser* in which he claimed to have evidence that Jonson accused Ford of stealing the play from Shakespeare.[4]

Two plays of the early nineteenth century, however, show some indebtedness to Ford. *The Kinsmen of Naples*, published anonymously in 1821,[5] carries the following Advertisement:

This Tragedy was originally taken from the Author's general recollection of the plot and characters of Ford's 'Witch

[1] J. Genest, *Some Account of the English Stage*, Bath 1832, iv, 197-8.
[2] *Ibid.*, iv, 243-5.   [3] Sargeaunt, pp. 170-1.   [4] See above, p. 108, n. 1.
[5] The authorship is something of a puzzle. The play was published along with *Conrad: or, The Usurper*, as 'By The Author of Tancred'. *Tancred*, a tale, was published in 1819 as by the author of *Conrad*, which had perhaps already been acted at Birmingham. The British Museum Catalogue and S. A. Tannenbaum's *John Ford (A Concise Bibliography)*, New York 1941, give the author as Alfred Bunn. Yet the Advertisement to the whole volume in which *The Kinsmen* and *Conrad* appeared thanks Mrs Bunn for her acting in *Conrad* and Mr Bunn for extensive help with that play: 'in addition to the benefit which the Tragedy derived from the emendations of his elegant pen, he gave it every advantage of scenery and music, which it could have received from a London Theatre'. Allardyce Nicoll, *A History of Early Nineteenth Century Drama 1800-1850*, 1930, ii, 434, gives *Conrad* and *The Kinsmen* under 'Unknown Authors'. As *Grove's Dictionary of Music and Musicians* (Fifth Edition, 1954, i, 1014) asserts that there is 'remarkably poor poetry' in Bunn's operatic libretti, he would not seem a likely author for the fairly respectable verse of *The Kinsmen*.

of Edmonton'; but the suggestions of friends induced so many alterations, as in a great measure to destroy the resemblance. The double marriage is the only incident which was retained from the old play: it was considered necessary, in order to heighten the stage effect, to give a stronger contrast in the females than is to be found in Ford.

Indeed there is little connection with Ford and Dekker's play. Lorenzo, Prince of Naples, has secretly married the peasant-girl Viola. His father persuades him to marry Olympia, sister of the Prince of Parma, under the pretence that Parma has a hold over his life. Viola comes to the city and discovers Lorenzo's second marriage. All ends in disaster. The author is clearly right in seeing only the double marriage as common to the two plays.

The Advertisement to the volume containing *Conrad* and *The Kinsmen* says that the late Miss O'Neil had been interested in staging *The Kinsmen* but died before it could be staged.

Professor Davril has pointed out the relationship between *Love's Sacrifice* and the *Mirandola* (1821) of Barry Cornwall (Bryan W. Procter).[1] This play, which was acted at Covent Garden on 9 January 1821,[2] has a central situation with some resemblance to that of Ford's play. The Duke of Mirandola has married Isidora, who was formerly betrothed to his son Guido; Guido has been thought dead, but learns of the marriage when he returns to court; he and Isidora are virtuous and acquiesce in the situation, but the Duke comes upon them at their farewell meeting, assumes their guilt, and has Guido executed. Isabella, the Duke's sister, is responsible for making him believe in Isidora's infidelity, and in this her function in the play is close to that of the Duke's sister, Fiormonda, in *Love's Sacrifice*. Another reminiscence

---

[1] Davril, p. 478.
[2] Allardyce Nicoll, *A History of Early Nineteenth Century Drama 1800-1850*, ii, 273.

of Ford here is that the Duke's first wife was called Bianca, and in the list of dramatis personae that name is also given, through perhaps a significant error, to the innkeeper's wife who is in the play called Beatrice. The play is not close to Ford except in these superficial matters, but it is worth noting that Barry Cornwall's *Dramatic Scenes and Other Poems* (1819) includes a playlet called *The Broken Heart*: it shows the grief and death of Jeronymo who, returning home after a long absence, finds his love Sylvestra married to another: evidently here the playwright had Orgilus and Penthea in mind.

(iii) *1890–1955*

As we should expect, the play of Ford most frequently performed in recent years is *'Tis Pity She's a Whore*. The earliest modern performance was that of Maeterlinck's adaptation[1] at the Théâtre de l'Œuvre in Paris on 6 November 1894.[2] It was not until 1923 that the English text was acted, in a Phoenix Society production, on January 28 and 29, with Ion Swinley as Giovanni and Miss Moyna MacGill as Annabella.[3] Then a French translation by Mr Georges Pillement was produced by Mr Charles Dullin at the Atelier in Paris in 1934, and it was apparently the same text that was given at the Théâtre Verlaine in 1948.[4] The original play was acted at the Arts Theatre, London, on 30 December 1934[5] and (with Mr Donald Wolfit as Giovanni) at the Arts Theatre, Cambridge, on 13 May 1940.[6] The most recent revival was at the Nottingham Playhouse in 1955.

The Broken Heart was one of the seventeenth-century plays revived by William Poel. His production was given at St George's Hall, London, on 11 June 1898. There was a

[1] See above, p. 15, n. 1.   [2] Sargeaunt, p. 171.   [3] *Ibid.*, p. 171.
[4] Davril, p. 500. It is not clear from Davril whether the later of these performances used Mr Pillement's translation, which was published, along with a translation of *Love's Sacrifice*, in 1925.
[5] Sargeaunt, p. 173.   [6] Davril, p. 500.

good deal of abridgement, the omissions including the scene
of Orgilus's suicide.[1] In November 1904 the play was given
by the Mermaid Society at the Royalty Theatre.[2]

The Witch of Edmonton was revived by the Phoenix
Society in London in 1921, and at the Old Vic (produced by
Mr Michel Saint-Denis, with Dame Edith Evans as Mother
Sawyer, Mr Marius Goring as Frank and Miss Beatrix
Lehmann as Winnifred) in 1936.[3]

The Spanish Gipsy was revived by William Poel at St
George's Hall, London, on 5 April 1898. A prologue by
Swinburne was written for this occasion.[4]

One fairly close imitation and one adaptation should also
be noted in this period. In 1892 John William Aizlewood
published *Warbeck A Historical Play in Two Parts Partly
founded on the Perkin Warbeck of Ford*. In his preface Aizlewood stated:

> The following tragedy, mostly written more than five years
> ago, was first inspired by a reading of Lord Bacon's *History of
> King Henry the Seventh*. It is also partly based on the *Perkin
> Warbeck* of John Ford, published in 1634, though mainly
> conceived, and the Prologue written, before I knew of that
> play's existence.

The length of this work (a dramatic Prologue and two five
act Parts) would make performance almost unthinkable,
and Aizlewood indicated that he had not attempted to adapt
himself to 'present theatrical needs'. In Part I he is closest to
Ford in Clifford's betrayal of Stanley. In Part II, when
James and Warbeck are invading Northumberland, Warbeck's reluctance to pillage the country and James's growing
impatience are obviously derived from Ford, although
Aizlewood makes Warbeck disingenuous in his conduct
here, as Ford does not. The central figure, as handled by

[1] Robert Speaight, *William Poel and the Elizabethan Revival*, 1954,
pp. 128-30.   [2] Sargeaunt, p. 171.
[3] *The Jacobean and Caroline Stage*, iii, 272; *The Times*, 9 December
1936.   [4] Robert Speaight, *op. cit.*, p. 127.

Aizlewood, persists in his pretensions to the end because he feels that he cannot disappoint Katherine's expectations of him: this makes for a conventional romanticism which is remote from the subtle portrait of the hero that Ford gives us. In Aizlewood, moreover, Warbeck's manner is generally pert rather than princely. We are bound to feel that this play has not preserved much that is worth while in Ford: it is a fairly characteristic piece of Victorian neo-Elizabethanism, written with diligence and some dignity; it does not affront, but its cumulative effect is wearisome and over-obvious.

In 1921 was published *The Duchess of Pavy*, an adaptation of *Love's Sacrifice* by Samuel A. Eliot, Jr.[1] In this version the Duke is suspicious (and, we are told, 'degenerate') from the beginning of the play. The sub-plots are omitted, including that showing Fiormonda's passion for Fernando: this makes her animus against the lovers unmotivated. The adaptor runs together the scene where Bianca comes to Fernando's bed and the scene where their love-making is interrupted by the Duke's return: he thus altogether misses the shrewd presentation of Bianca's recklessness when she feels she has conquered temptation ('Speak, shall I steal a kiss? believe me, my lord, I long'). Altogether the compression in this version diminishes the play's power of conviction, and brings it away from Ford's world and nearer to that of Wilde's *A Florentine Tragedy* and Stephen Phillips's *Paolo and Francesca*. Though the attempt to bring *Love's Sacrifice* back to the theatre was commendable, this adaptation is destructive of the play's character and quality. It did not reach the stage: the adaptor's preface tells us that 'in a yet shorter version than the present' it was 'rehearsed at the Cincinatti Art Theater in 1917, but has not yet attained performance'.[2]

---

[1] *Little Theater Classics Volume Three*, Boston 1921.

[2] In addition to the performances on the professional stage noted in this section, there have been some amateur and broadcast performances of Ford plays.

INDEX

DATE DUE